His Darling Wife,
Evelyn

The Autobiography
of Mrs. Oral Roberts

Evelyn Roberts

G.K.HALL&CO.

 Boston, Massachusetts

1977

Library of Congress Cataloging in Publication Data

Roberts, Evelyn, 1917-
  His darling wife, Evelyn.

  Large print ed.
  1. Roberts, Evelyn, 1917-   2. Roberts, Oral.
3. Clergymen's wives — Oklahoma — Tulsa — Biography.
4. Tulsa, Okla. — Biography. 5. Methodist Church —
Clergy — Biography. 6. Clergy — Oklahoma — Tulsa —
Biography. 7. Large type books. I. Title.
[BX8495.R52A3 1977] 269'.2'0924 [B] 77-1416
ISBN 0-8161-6469-X

A James Wade/Damascus House Book, published in
Large Print by arrangement with Dial Press

Set in Compugraphic 18 pt English Times

*Dedicated to Oral,
who so lovingly nudged
me to write this book,
and to Rebecca, Ronnie,
Richard, and Roberta,
who allowed me to include
personal incidents that
happened in their lives*

Contents

Introduction

A twelve-year-old girl once came up to me at the close of a meeting in which Oral had preached. She shyly asked me, "How does it feel to live with a man of God?"

Her question stunned me for a moment and I responded almost without thinking, "I can't imagine living any other kind of life except one with *this* man of God — Oral Roberts."

For the past thirty-five years, Oral has introduced me to people as his "darling wife, Evelyn." That's all I've ever wanted to be . . . his inspiration, his helpmate, his comfort, his wife, and the mother of his children.

When we married, we vowed loyalty to each other "in sickness and in health, rich or poor." We've lived our vows! We've had rock-bottom times and we've had mountaintop times. Together, we've learned a great deal about God's love and living by faith . . . about giving to others and about living an abundant Christian life.

This is my story. And because Oral Roberts is my husband, this is *our* story. I hope you find Jesus in these pages and that our experiences in Him will be a blessing to you.

Your friend always,
Evelyn

A Huge, Happy, Hilarious Heart

It was summer. And summers in our family meant camp meetings. The summer of 1936 was no exception. That year the camp meeting, which amounted to a religious retreat, was held in Sulphur, Oklahoma.

Mamma and Daddy packed up the car and my five brothers and sisters (two more were born later) and me — and off we went.

It was natural for me to take along my guitar. There was always a young people's music group at camp meeting. Anyone with a guitar, violin, or horn could come and join in. One didn't even have to have any special talent — just a desire. I played in church all the time, so I took my guitar along to the first meeting. The "orchestra" was already formed at the front when I

1

arrived and there was only one empty chair left.

I sat down and when I looked around, my heart turned a flip, for sitting beside me was a handsome young man with black hair and blue eyes. He said, "Who are you? I've never met you before."

"I'm Evelyn Lutman from Westville."

We sat together playing our guitars every night all week, and he never asked me for a date. Not once.

He asked questions all right, but not the right kind.

"What do you work at?"

"I'm a schoolteacher."

"Really?" He seemed impressed. I was nineteen and had already taught one year of country school.

One night he came rushing in late — shoved me in the ribs and said, "Hey, does my hair look like it's been combed?" I thought, My, what an impulsive guy! I looked at him — his tie crooked and his hair looking as if it had had an accident with a comb. I told him he looked very nice, but in my heart I was saying, "You *will* look very nice a few years from now

2

when you are my husband!"

Nobody could convince me then, or now, that "love at first sight" is impossible. Love for this tall handsome man named Oral Roberts had hit me like a thunderbolt.

He looked *exactly* like the person I had always imagined marrying. In flesh and blood, he was the mental dream of the person I envisioned my future husband to be. I didn't know he was a minister or anything about him. But I knew he *looked* exactly as I wanted *my* husband to look.

I was so sure of my feelings that I wrote in my diary, "Tonight I met my future husband. He is tall and handsome. His name is Oral Roberts. Someday I intend to marry him." But I couldn't just walk up to him and say, "Hey, I want to marry you," now could I? Especially when he didn't seem to feel the same way.

I sang a solo one night: "His Eye Is on the Sparrow." I never did have a very good voice, and Oral didn't overlook the fact. He told the person next to him, "That's a pretty girl up there, but she sure can't sing."

Oral had come to camp meeting for more of God, not for girls. He had recently

3

been healed by the Lord of tuberculosis, and he came to the camp meeting seeking to know more about God's Holy Spirit. That's all he had on his mind. I was just another guitar-playing schoolteacher to him — but one who knew what she wanted when she saw it!

Oral was coming. Two years had passed and now I was going to see him again.

It was a hot, humid September afternoon. I was sitting at my teacher's desk in a country schoolhouse in Texas — busily planning the story hour for the last class session of the day. The children were out at recess playing.

Suddenly they came rushing in, all shouting at once, "Oh, Miss Evelyn, Miss Evelyn, your boyfriend has come."

I had told the children I was expecting a guest that day and that I wanted them to be very nice. When they saw it was a gentleman guest, they put two and two together and came up with "boyfriend."

Correspondent would have been a better word since the United States Postal Service had been entirely responsible for our reunion. On my twenty-first birthday I had received a little package in the mail. I hurriedly tore the brown paper, thinking it was a gift from home. Instead, my eyes fell on a book entitled *Salvation by the Blood* by Oral Roberts. I looked inside and found a little note: "Congratulations on your twenty-first birthday. Please accept this little book from me. I trust it will bless your soul."

That note was like a bombshell dropped out of the heavens. I stopped everything and read the book. Then I did something I had wanted to do for a long time — I fell on my knees and talked to God.

I sent a note to Oral thanking him for the book and for remembering me on my birthday. Immediately a letter came from him asking that we carry on a correspondence. From the way the correspondence began there was no indication that our letters would ever be other than friendly. He described his ministry as that of a very young, beginning evangelist and even sent whole sermons he had prepared, for me to read.

Then came the day that I received a never-to-be-forgotten letter. As usual, I was thrilled to see Oral's letter on the table when I came in after a long day of teaching. I quickly opened it and began to read. "Who knows," Oral wrote, "we may spend the next fifty years of our lives together."

I read these words over and over. If such an idea were in his mind, he should have confided it to the secret pages of a diary (as I had) — not just scrawled it out coldly without a word about love!

At one of our first meetings he had blurted out the question about his hair, and now without any declaration of love, he wanted to spend the next fifty years with me. What kind of person is he, I wondered.

I sat down and wrote him just what I thought of such a presumption. After I mailed the letter, I began to wish that I hadn't. Being unable to recall it, I hastily wrote another letter asking him to forgive me and to please disregard the first letter.

The damage was done, however, before the second letter arrived. Promptly, I received an airmail special-delivery reply. "You needn't worry," he wrote. "If you think I would want to spend the rest of my life with you, you are badly mistaken."

Well, by then I knew we either had a bad case of "true love" that doesn't run smoothly, or I should burn my diary. I felt terrible about what had happened between us and I wondered if he would ever write to me again. Out of all this I learned two things about Oral's nature: He will never go where he is not wanted, but he isn't one to retreat when he feels the Lord wants him to pursue something or someone.

Another letter soon came from Oral suggesting that we both forget we had written such ugly letters. As for me, I was glad to forget them. He asked, "May I come to see you?"

I told him "yes" and invited him to spend the weekend with my grandparents who lived about 150 miles from where I was teaching.

And now he had come. I smoothed the wrinkles from my cotton skirt and went out to greet him. I looked at him and the old thoughts went racing through my mind, He is exactly right. He *is* what I want. He's *exactly* what I want.

He was tall and slender, and in his new pearl-gray suit, he was the handsomest man I'd ever seen. He was leaning against a brand-new car — a Chevrolet roadster. It was a beautiful blue car.

He smiled at me and nearly took my breath away.

And then I looked again. His mother was sitting in the car! He hadn't told me he was bringing his mother.

I had never met Oral's mother, but I didn't have much time to panic. Oral was here — and I was so glad to see him I was willing to take him with whatever or whomever he happened to have along!

I wanted to run to him and kiss him hello — but with his mother in the car and a playground filled with staring third and fourth graders, what could I do? We shook hands.

I said, "I can't leave for forty-five minutes. You're both welcome to come inside and sit in the schoolroom with me while I finish my last class." His mother decided to wait in the car, but just as I began the story hour, in walked Oral and I absolutely came unglued. I have no idea what the story was nor how I got through that period. I do remember letting the children out early, and to them that was something special.

We drove back to my apartment to pick up my suitcase. I was living with two other teachers in a two-story frame boardinghouse. I introduced Oral to the housekeeper and then we went upstairs to get my luggage.

And that's when he grabbed me and hugged and kissed me for the first time.

When we got to my grandparents' home in Texas, Oral's mother and I shared a bedroom. I was glad to share a room with Mama Roberts as it gave me time to get acquainted with her. She questioned me quite a bit about my goals in life and about how much I liked her son. Mama Roberts had a pretty good idea of how serious Oral was about "that girl in Texas," and she wanted to be sure he didn't make a mistake.

I knew she was looking me over closely,

but I felt it was her privilege and I didn't resent it. Besides, I was watching her very closely, too. I wanted to see what it would be like to live in this family.

Oral had not proposed yet, but I knew he would. I had known *that* for two years. I just didn't know how or when.

Every chance Oral and I had, we tried to get away from my grandparents' house. Most of the time his mother and my grandmother tagged along. We couldn't seem to shake them.

We went on a picnic — and they went, too. We took a boat trip and they came along. We decided to go to the Gulf of Mexico and fish, and they went right along. In order to get away, we took our fishing poles to the end of the long jetty that pushed out from the beach into the ocean. My grandmother was afraid of deep water and so was his mother, so that seemed the best way of escape. We climbed down on the rocks next to the water and really had an opportunity to get acquainted.

We didn't watch those fishing lines very much; in fact we didn't catch a thing but each other. We talked and talked and I felt I'd known him for a hundred years. On the way home, Oral insisted that his mother ride with my grandparents in their car. Oral told them to go ahead and that we'd be home shortly. So they went, and we sat in the car parked on the sandbar and talked. He told me how he planned to someday travel to Israel and minister there.

And then all of a sudden he said, "Evelyn, my huge, happy, hilarious heart is throbbing tumultuously, tremendously, triumphantly in a lasting, long-lived love for you. As I gaze into your beauteous, bounteous, beaming eyes, I am literally lost in a daring, delightful dream in which your fair, felicitous, fancy-filled face is ever present like a colossal, comprehensive constellation. Will you be my sweet, smiling, soulful, satisfied spouse?"

I couldn't believe my ears! That was no way to propose marriage. So I looked at him and said, "Listen here, if you're trying to propose to me, do it in the English language."

"Honey, I really *am* asking you to marry me," he said.

And I protested, "Oral, you don't know

11

very much about me."

"I know much more than you think. I have asked everybody about you."

But he didn't know all. I said, "Since I've been here in Texas I haven't been as close to the Lord as I once was. I gave my heart to the Lord when I was twelve, Oral, and I never had a desire to be rebellious or to miss church."

(I loved going to church. I could never understand my children when they rebelled about going to Sunday school and church as teen-agers. Of course, their protests didn't help them. They went anyway. But I couldn't understand *why* they didn't want to go. I had never lost my enthusiasm for going to Sunday school and church. But when I left home and began to teach, I felt I had to get "in" with the community people — to be friendly and do the things they did.)

"One of the favorite family and community projects in this town is dancing, Oral. I've been going to their dances. I've started going to movies, too. When I was at home, I never went to movies or dances, and I've never smoked or had a drink.

I've been taught that these things are serious sins. And I love to dance, Oral. I picked it up the quickest you've ever seen in your life. And I feel, well, I've just left the Lord out of my life. He is not first anymore. I have written to my church back home and asked that my name be taken out of the church membership book because I feel I've wandered away from the Lord and have done things a church member shouldn't do.

"Sometimes during a stormy night I pull the covers up over my head and pray, 'O God, I know I'm doing wrong. Please don't let me die until I'm right with You.' But I haven't been willing to turn loose of these things, Oral. I don't think I'm the type of wife you want. When I met you I was, but now I've done things I'm not proud of."

I loved Oral and wanted him for my husband, but I felt I had to be honest with him.

Oral took my hand and patted it and said, "Evelyn, you *will* be right with God. You know the Lord. You'll never get away from Him."

"No, I don't want to get away from Him. I know that there will be a time in my life when I will belong absolutely to God. But right now I'm not and I have to be honest with you."

He said, "I'm not afraid." And we left it like that. He didn't ask me to repent or pray. He changed the subject.

We spent about two hours in the car discussing our future plans. Oral shared with me his hopes, his dreams, his ambitions in life. That weekend was to be our first date, only date, and last date, so we had a lot to talk about. He had to tell me all of the things we might be involved in if we married and how he felt about God and life, and of course, he wanted to know what I wanted out of life, too.

With all sincerity and tender love I said, "Oral, where you go, I will go. Your ministry will be my ministry and your God, my God!"

(When we got ready to leave, we found we were stuck in the sandbar. We had to find somebody to help us free the car. That part wasn't so romantic. . . .)

The next day, Saturday, we read about

an evangelist who was holding tent meetings in a little town about ten miles away. Oral said, "It would be nice to go there to church tonight. Would you like to go?"

I agreed and of course everybody else wanted to go, too. My grandparents, my aunt and uncle, and Oral's mother went with us to hear this man speak. I don't remember his name or what he preached about, but at one point in the service he asked for people to come to the altar to rededicate their lives to the Lord. Everybody was standing when he asked that. Oral didn't say a word to me. He just stepped back for me to step out into the aisle. And I did. My grandmother came and knelt beside me — she wanted to make sure that I didn't get something I wasn't supposed to have.

So I knelt there and prayed. Oral's mother knelt on the other side of the altar facing me and I shall never forget what she prayed: "Lord, Evelyn is your child and she hasn't done anything bad, so you just take her back tonight."

It broke my heart to hear her say that and I really renewed my whole commitment to the Lord. I bawled up a storm. Grandmother couldn't understand why I was crying so hard. She kept saying, "Evelyn, are you *sure* you're all right?"

Oral stood by and smiled.

When we got to the car, he reached over and patted me on the knee and said, "Now I'm *sure* I want you." We made plans to be married the following June.

All the way back to my schoolhouse in Riviera my heart was singing. It was I who had the "huge, happy, hilarious heart."

I was engaged to Oral. And my commitment to God was renewed.

Preachers
Were Out of My Line

To say that I was lonely after Oral went back to Oklahoma would be putting it mildly. Along with loneliness I was filled with anxiety. Though I loved Oral, I still did not know him very well. I had many questions and doubts.

In the first place, preachers in general were out of my line.

I had no intention as a young girl of marrying a minister and I certainly wasn't attracted to Oral *because* he was a preacher. I knew the trials and tribulations of a preacher's life. I didn't want any part of that kind of life.

Then my Grandmother Wingate, whose opinion I valued dearly, threw a terrible fit when I told her I was going to marry Oral. I went to spend a weekend with my grandparents and we were having breakfast out on the screened porch when I broke the news to her. I might as well have been the queen of England abdicating the throne. She cried and cried, "Oh, Evelyn, I had such high hopes for you. Now they're all gone!"

My grandfather, bless his heart, took my part — as he had so many times in the past when Grandmother was not pleased with my actions — and he settled her down so we could at least have a sensible discussion.

It deeply distressed my grandmother when I held firm to my belief that Oral was the one for me. She wanted me to marry someone with a high social standing and a business profession, and she couldn't see that Oral had either of those qualities.

I began to receive advice from my friends and other relatives, too — all negative. My fellow teachers teased me about being a poor preacher's wife. And even when they were serious they said, "Oh, Evelyn, you don't want to marry a *preacher,* do you?"

It wasn't as if Oral Roberts was the first

man to propose to me. He certainly wasn't.

Between the camp meeting when I met Oral and the weekend he proposed, two other men had approached me with marriage on their minds.

One of them was about ten years older than I was. He said to me, "I admire you, Evelyn, and I'm at the age when I need a wife. You are the kind of woman I need. You know I live with my folks who are elderly, and soon all they have will be mine and yours. I want you for my wife."

"I'm flattered," I replied, "and I appreciate what you are saying. I admire you and I enjoy being with you, but I'm not *really* the type of wife you need. I've been a born-again Christian and that's what I plan to be again. I know the Lord has something for me to do someday."

"Well, I'd never hamper you in anything you wanted to do for the Lord."

"I know, but you wouldn't fully understand. You deserve a wife who deeply loves you and will honor you."

I always felt that I would meet Oral again, or meet somebody else exactly like him. Even though I felt alienated from

God, I had another feeling in those days that my life was not always going to be the way it was. I would have been afraid to marry someone who had never known the joy of salvation.

I dated another young man an entire summer and then he moved away. One day he came back on his way to a business appointment in a nearby town. He called to ask me if I would ride over with him. I did. He had a brand-new pickup truck and had opened his own business, which appeared to be successful. When we had dated, we had laughed a lot and had good times together.

On the way to the appointment, he said, "Evelyn, I've really come to ask you a very important question. I want you to be my wife."

"Well, I'm going to have to be very truthful with you," I said. "I don't love you as a wife should love a husband. We've had fun together. I've enjoyed being with you and talking with you, but I'm not the type of wife you need. You need somebody who will get involved in your work and I don't think I could be."

"I don't understand. I'll provide a good home for you. I'll build you any kind of home you'd like. I need you and I've come to ask you to marry me and go back with me."

"You need a wife who will give you the *love* you deserve and I don't love you in that way."

He went home and several weeks later I received a letter from his new bride. I had forgotten to give him back his class ring when he moved away. She wrote, "Evelyn, my husband has told me all about you and you must be a wonderful person. He's had nothing but good things to say about you. He forgot to get his class ring from you and I wonder if you'd mind sending it? I want you to know that any time you come through our town, you're welcome in our home."

That was one of the sweetest letters I ever received. I don't know that I could have written a letter like that to one of Oral's girl friends after we married.

Speaking of Oral — that was another area in question. He was miles away in

21

Oklahoma. What about all of his girl friends there? And believe me, Oral had the girl friends, each of whom thought she was God-appointed to be his wife. In one of his meetings, seventeen young girls came to the altar to accept the Lord, and one old man and one old woman!

Mama Roberts told me many times, "Evelyn, I preserved Oral for you. When I met you in Texas, I knew immediately that Oral was going to marry you. When he got home and the girls started chasing after him and criticizing his decision, I just showed them the door. I told them he'd found the girl he was going to marry and I wouldn't let them change his mind. I really saved him for you."

All of these anxieties came rushing to my mind during the weeks after Oral proposed. My mother was the only person who encouraged me in my decision. And this was strange, I thought, because years before when we moved from Missouri to Oklahoma Mamma had voiced a fear that one of her children might marry an Indian. Oral is part Cherokee and Choctaw.

I had accepted Oral's proposal before I

had heard him preach. Knowing my mother had heard Oral, I wrote to her and asked what she thought about him. Mamma wrote back and said, "Evelyn, you need not worry. He's a good preacher now, as young as he is. [He was twenty-one.] What will he be in a few years?"

But did I want to be a preacher's wife? Were my grandmother and my friends right? Was there somebody else in my future who would be better? Would Oral change his mind? Should I wait to know him better?

I was all alone with my questions in Texas. All alone, that is, except for God. I did a lot of praying. Finally, one night I prayed, "Lord, I am six hundred miles away from my future husband. I don't know what is going on where Oral is. When I listen to my friends and relatives all I hear is, 'No, don't. You'll be sorry.' But my heart keeps crying, 'Yes.' If it is Your will for us to marry, then let it work out for us according to Your will. If I shouldn't marry Oral Roberts, break it up now."

After I prayed, the anxiety left me. Peace filled my heart. I could not wait to know Oral Roberts better. God knew Oral and I knew God would keep me in His perfect will.

Just for Me

Part of the reason I didn't have a great desire to be a preacher's wife was that I was raised in a preacher's home. Daddy held revival meetings, but it was during the Great Depression and he also farmed to make ends meet. One time, he had to join the WPA (Works Projects Administration) and I remember how embarrassed I was.

My sister Ruth and I traveled with Daddy to meetings. She played the violin, I played the guitar, and Daddy preached. People would always give us food, but there was very little money. I'd say to myself, "I'm going to marry a man who has a job and makes *money*. I'm not going to half starve to death. Just because I've been brought up in this kind of a family doesn't mean I'm going to live this way all my life." I had had all the old poor stuff I wanted, and I knew there had to be a better life for *my* children.

I call him Daddy, but that first preacher in my life was really my stepfather.

My mother and my own father divorced when I was four and my sister Ruth was two (we were his only children). They divorced because my father was an alcoholic. He became a different person under the influence of alcohol.

I remember going to him one morning while he was reading the paper and my mother was cooking breakfast, only to have him push me against the red-hot stove. He had been drunk the evening before and was still recovering; a two-year-old child hungry for his affection was not eagerly received. I remember that he and my mother had quite an argument afterward. He had abused her, too, several times, but only when he was drunk.

My father's drinking had such an effect on me at that early age that I've had a terrible time all my life being tolerant of people who drink. It makes me furious to think that anybody would want to drink something that makes him take leave of his senses. I'm convinced alcohol is a tool that Satan uses. I have had to pray very hard, and read the Beatitudes many times, to be more understanding toward people who use alcohol. Alcohol ruined my home and tore my family apart, and it's difficult for me to be tolerant.

I never kept close contact with my father. He remarried soon after my parents divorced. I saw him once when I was about twelve, when we went to Missouri to visit my grandparents. One day we were sitting in the car in my grandparents' town and my mother said to me, "Evelyn, there goes your father." She pointed to a man strolling down the sidewalk.

I can't explain how I felt. I had a strong urge to say something to him. But I also knew he was a stranger and he wouldn't know me. I didn't say anything to him.

When I was in college, Ruth wrote that our father had tuberculosis and that he didn't know the Lord. I had such a burden for him that I began to write to him.

I told him I was sorry I had not had any contact with him through my growing-up years, and that I was a Christian. He wrote two or three letters to me. He said he still loved Ruth and me.

I felt a responsibility for my father since I knew the Lord as my personal Savior and I wasn't sure he did. And I felt compassion knowing that he had tuberculosis.

Oral and I were in Georgia conducting a crusade when I received the message my father had died. I felt I had been robbed of an opportunity to tell him face to face what Jesus meant in my life and of His healing power. I wanted to be assured that he knew Jesus and I really blamed myself for not having witnessed personally to him. I asked the Lord many times, Why? Finally, the Lord seemed to say to me, "Evelyn, I can handle things. I don't really need your help." The burden lifted as I began to trust in His wisdom.

When my parents divorced, I went to live with my grandparents part of the time, but most of the time I stayed with my mother. Mamma would let us spend our summers with our grandparents. They were good to us and, of course, I loved them dearly. They seemed to take the place of my father.

When Mamma remarried, Ruth and I went to live with her and my new stepfather. The summer they married, we lived on my grandfather's farm in Missouri, close to the Lake of the Ozarks. Part of our land was on one side of the Osage River, and part of it was on the hilly land on the other side. There was a little place where the river could be easily forded by a wagon and we planted crops on nearby Corn Hill. Someone that summer built a little brush arbor on Corn Hill to hold meetings.

Do you know what a brush arbor is? I forget sometimes that we don't have them now. In those days, people would cut down young trees and trim them for poles and plant them in the ground. Then they would take smaller poles and make a lattice of them on top. They would cover the lattice with branches of trees to make a roof. Then they would take blocks of wood and put planks of lumber on them for seats. Kerosine lanterns would be hung on the posts — and that was a brush arbor. It would be expanded as big as necessary for the crowds and it cost nothing to build.

People would come from all over the county to brush-arbor meetings, bringing their entire families with them. In those days people sometimes had large families, and the mothers would bring quilts for the children to sleep on during evening services.

One day a neighbor rode over to tell Daddy that there was an old woman named Granny Hubbs who "shouted" every night during the meetings on Corn Hill. Daddy said to Mamma, "Let's saddle the horses and put the girls behind us, and go over tonight and see this woman who shouts."

So we went that night. And Mamma and Daddy enjoyed the service so much that they went the next night. Daddy said the only reason he went was to hear Granny Hubbs shout. But they wound up going every night and they both accepted the Lord during that brush-arbor revival meeting. It didn't seem to be the minister who was having an effect on them, it was old Granny Hubbs's shouting!

After my parents accepted Christ, our lives changed considerably. Our friends changed. Our habits changed.

Daddy, as I had come to call him, had an insatiable hunger for God. He wouldn't allow any Christian meeting to be held anywhere near us without our attending. He read every Christian book he could lay his hands on. He sent for many books through the mail and read them during every spare hour. Amy Semple McPherson was in her heyday at that time. She had just built her temple in Los Angeles and I remember that Daddy sent for her monthly magazine.

When it came each month he would weep. Its message was so powerful and his heart was so hungry for more of God that he couldn't keep back the tears of joy.

Daddy's sister lived in Coffeyville, Kansas, and a few months after my parents were converted she wrote that people in her church were falling into a trance — and when they came out of the trance they were speaking in languages nobody understood. She wrote that the Lord was doing something marvelous in their church

— something they had neither seen nor heard before — and that it was just like the Book of Acts.

Daddy began to read Acts and he found where, on the day of Pentecost, people had received this same experience of speaking in strange languages. So he said to Mamma, "I'm going up there, and I'm going to see what's going on."

Sure enough, when he got to Coffeyville, he found people falling under the power of God and speaking new languages. He was fascinated. He returned home and said, "We're locking up this house and we're moving to Coffeyville until I receive this experience." We did just that. Daddy rented an apartment in Coffeyville and arranged for someone to care for the crops. We lived in Coffeyville for a year until my father received the baptism in the Holy Spirit.

I was only six years old then but I remember the little church and the Spirit-filled people and the joy that emanated from them.

When we moved back to the farm, Daddy traveled the countryside looking for someone who believed as he did in the Holy Spirit's baptism. He wanted to find someone to come and preach in our community. Finally he found a young man in Oklahoma named Dean Smith. Reverend Smith was a full-gospel preacher. He and his wife came to our little community and brought with them a young girl to play the organ and sing. Her name was Minnie Pryor. I remember her so well. As she sang and played the old pump organ the joy of the Lord shone in her countenance. As a result of the meetings a full-gospel church was founded and we were among its first members.

When I was about eight, Daddy heard about a Christian school in Checotah, Oklahoma. He said, "I don't want our children to go *only* to public schools. [By this time there were four of us, J.D., Kathleen, Ruth, and me.] I think they should also go to Christian schools. And I'd like to take some Bible courses."

So, we moved to Checotah that summer. Daddy fixed a shade over the back part of the truck for us children and Mamma gave us quilts to sit on. It took us two days to drive from Missouri to Checotah.

My Wingate grandparents felt we were moving to the edge of the world. Grandmother cried and hugged me, saying, "Evelyn, if you don't like it out there, come back and stay with Dampy [my grandfather] and me."

In the fall we started school. Mamma was housemother in the girls' dorm and Daddy took Bible courses.

Families came to Checotah from all over Oklahoma to enroll their children in the Christian school there. Some came who had just struck it rich in the oil boom at Seminole. Others were poor people like us.

Sometime later, there was a disagreement among the faculty members and the school became divided. Finally the school closed and we went with some of the faculty members to start a new school in Arkansas. Mamma became the housemother at different times in both the boys' and girls' dormitories there. I remember how the students flocked to our apartment to talk to Mamma. My mother has a strong character and a strong physique. You know by the tone of her voice that she means what she says. Yet she speaks with kindness. Young people have always enjoyed being with her.

The mountains and clear springs of Arkansas were beautiful to me. My sister and I carried many buckets of sparkling, cool water up the hill from our nearby spring. I still get thirsty for that sweet, pure taste.

Ola Pryor, Minnie's sister, was one of the girls at the school in Arkansas. Ola was six years older than I but she'd go on long walks with me and we would talk together. She was a very special friend. (Years later both Minnie and Ola were to have sons who would join us in my husband's ministry and the founding of Oral Roberts University.)

We met people from around the world while we lived in Arkansas. The school hosted visiting evangelists and held camp meetings in addition to school sessions. It seemed I was always in church or at a religious meeting.

When I was twelve, there was a very special meeting. A young woman who attended the school played a violin and sang. She would play alto on the violin and sing the melody, and vice versa. One evening she sang a song I will never forget. It was about Jesus, and how He went all the way to Calvary for me.

I had attended church since I was six years old, and the preacher's message that night was nothing new to me. I can't even remember what he said, but when this girl sang her song I felt that Jesus climbed that hill and was nailed to the cross *just for me.* I've always felt that if a person can just get a mental picture of Jesus his or her heart will be touched. I felt I saw Jesus on the cross that night and it broke me to pieces. As much as a child of twelve can, I made a commitment of my life to Him. It was the turning point of my life.

The seven years of Bible study I received at the two Christian schools I attended were invaluable to me. Not only did I accept Jesus Christ as Savior and Lord during those years, I received the baptism in the Holy Spirit and became firmly grounded in the Word of God.

After the school in Arkansas disbanded,

due to lack of funds, Dad scouted several towns looking for a church that was strong in Jesus and alive with the Holy Spirit. If we couldn't attend a Christian school, he wanted his children to be near a Christ-filled church. He finally moved us to Westville, Oklahoma, and we lived there until I graduated from high school. I owe much of my spiritual heritage to my stepfather. His remarkable determination to keep the family in a spiritual environment prepared me someday to meet Oral.

Although we were poor in material things, we certainly were never impoverished when it came to love or the blessings of God. The Spirit of Jesus in our home far outweighed the "riches" of many other families.

Ruth and I had six half brothers and sisters, J.D., Kathleen, Betty, Paul, Bobbie, and George. We were all brought up together. No one received any special treatment and I love my half brothers and half sisters as I love Ruth. Being the eldest, it seems I have taken care of all of them at one time or other.

Some of my favorite memories are of

Mamma baking bread. Twice a week she'd bake six loaves of bread and I can still smell that bread coming out of the oven. I couldn't wait to get a piece of it.

One night I made divinity candy. Now when my dad hunted 'possums, he'd save the oil from their hides and bottle it to use in softening the leather of the horse saddles and his old, heavy, work shoes. He put the 'possum oil on the back of the big range to keep it liquefied.

Unfortunately, this time he had put it in an empty vanilla bottle. When it came time to put the flavoring in my candy! . . . Well, you can guess what happened. The whole batch was ruined.

Ruth and I were especially close. We both loved going to church and studying the Bible. One of us always had to stay at home with the other children while my parents went to weeknight Bible study and we'd take turns. If there was a revival service, we'd fuss about which one of us had to stay home. Neither of us ever wanted to miss church.

My baby sister, Betty, was born during a tornado. When it came time for her to be born, my dad took the younger children into another room of the house and I was sent to the home of my schoolteacher. The sky looked so strange, almost yellowish. I was happy to go to my teacher's house because I admired her so much.

When I arrived she said, "You know, Evelyn, I believe we're going to have a storm." I dreaded storms, especially when I was away from the safety of home. Some boys were playing ball in the school yard next door and my teacher sent them home.

About that time the storm hit. The wind began to howl. We locked all the doors and windows, but my teacher told me to stand with my back against the door. The wind was blowing so fiercely that it looked as if it would blow the doors in. The teacher stood against the door at the other end of the house. The wind came from one side and then it twisted around and came from the other side.

My teacher kept saying, "The Lord will take care of us. He will, and we'll be fine." And sure enough we were. No one was killed, although some homes were torn up and roofs lost to the wind. I always tell Betty that she was born in a tornado and she's been one ever since.

As much as I believe anything, I believe God prepared me to marry Oral, and prepared Oral to marry me. Oral preaches a sermon about David and Goliath, and in it he points out how God allowed water to run for centuries over the five stones that David used. God knew in advance that those stones would be needed and he began "smoothing them out" years ahead of time. God is never surprised.

I had no idea as I grew up — as most girls don't — about what my future would hold. But looking back, it was during those years that God was shaping me like David's smooth stones for the man and the ministry that were to be my life.

Across the Hills . . .

Across the hills of Oklahoma, a little boy was also learning what it was like to be the child of a poor preacher. He, too, sought a career that had nothing to do with preaching.

Ellis Melvin Roberts was a Welsh farmer in Pontotoc County — a steward in the Methodist Church as was his father before him. He and his Cherokee-Choctaw Indian wife, Claudius Priscilla, had five children. The youngest they named Granville Oral.

Three months before their last baby was born, Mama Roberts received a call from a neighbor whose child was dying from pneumonia. The doctor said the baby wouldn't survive 'til morning. Crying, the neighbor called Mama to come and pray for the desperately ill child.

Although it was late in the evening and

the wind was blowing as it blows only in Oklahoma, Mama went. It was a two-mile walk across the fields and woods and as she walked alone, tired, and feeling awkward, she prayed, "God, I make You a vow. I ask you to heal my neighbor's child. When my child is born, I will give him to You."

Mama Roberts prayed for the sick child in the name of Jesus and his life was spared. For Mama, that settled the matter. She was going to have a son and he was going to be a minister. She was convinced.

It took some time though for Oral to be convinced.

In the first place, preachers don't stutter or stammer. And Oral did, badly. He couldn't even say his own name. The children at school, and his own relatives, laughed unmercifully at him until he became extremely self-conscious and shy. He trained himself to talk as little as possible.

In the second place, preachers were characteristically poor. Oral Roberts was sick and tired of being poor.

When Oral was just a child, Mama and

Papa Roberts went to a brush-arbor meeting held by a full-gospel preacher — very much like the meeting my parents attended — and they were converted and received the baptism in the Holy Spirit. Papa began to testify about his experiences and beliefs.

Papa was loving and kind. I don't think I ever heard him raise his voice at anyone. He was even-tempered and dependable but not very ambitious. He would pastor a church for a while and then "retire" or preach a revival and come home to rest until the groceries ran out and the rent was due. As a result, it was either feast or famine in the Robertses' home.

Oral has often told me the story of one evening in their home when Mama said to Vaden and Oral, "Boys, we don't have anything to eat tonight so we are going visiting for the church instead."

The three of them went up the street to visit old Sister Campbell, a widow who had several children. They got there just as the family was sitting down to supper. Sister Campbell said, "Oh, Sister Roberts, you are just in time to have supper with us."

But Mama's pride was too great and she said, "Oh, no, we are not hungry." It's a good thing she didn't ask Oral because he would have accepted her offer!

Before they left, they all had prayer together and Mama began praising the Lord for being so good to them. On the way home Vaden said, "Mama, why did you pray like that? You know God isn't very good to us. We haven't got anything to eat. Papa is off holding a revival and you wouldn't even let us eat at Sister Campbell's tonight."

Oral said, "Now, Vaden, you hush. God will take care of us. You just hush and see what the Lord will do."

Oral didn't have a doubt that God would take care of them. When they got home, Vaden ran up on the porch to open the door. He said, "Mama, there is something behind this door. I can't open it." Oral ran up to help him and together they pushed the door open. When they flipped on the light, they saw the biggest box of groceries ever!

Mama began to thank the Lord and the boys began to unpack the box. About midnight they had a supper of ham, fried potatoes, and homemade biscuits. But there were times the story didn't have such a happy ending and Vaden and Oral went to bed hungry.

One thing they *did* have in Oral's family was a lot of prayer. Oral often says that when he was small he thought Jesus lived with them because Mama and Papa talked to Him so much.

Mama and Papa had family prayer each night. They would include all the children in their prayers and never failed to call their names to the Lord.

They would pray, "And now, dear Lord, bless Elmer, bless Jewel, bless Vaden, and bless Oral. Keep them from all harm, accident, and danger. Keep them from the devil's power and keep Your hand upon their lives. Make them men and women who will stir the world."

Sometimes they would fail to call Oral's name, and he would get up, walk over, and say, "You didn't call my name to Jesus." They would get back down on their knees and mention his name. And as if to make up for what they had failed to do, they would take a little extra time to pray for him and tell the Lord what they wanted Him to do for Oral.

Papa and Mama believed their children were something special to God, and they wanted Him to put His hand upon them.

People would often look at the children and say, "Here is the one who is going to make his mark."

They meant Vaden, not Oral. Vaden has always had a wonderful personality. He was the favorite with everybody, and he was Oral's favorite, too.

Oral was frail in his body and when he got into any trouble, it was Vaden who would stand up for him. If Oral wanted something from Mama and Papa, Vaden always asked for it. When they were around people, everybody would always talk to Vaden.

Vaden never laughed at Oral. That wasn't true of other people.

Once on Vaden's birthday, some friends invited him to their house for birthday cake and homemade ice cream. They didn't invite Oral and it broke his heart. In about two hours he decided that he would go anyway. He put on his new suit and walked a half mile down the country road to their house. There he sat on the front porch until the people came out and invited him in.

People would often come up to Papa and say, "Brother Roberts, Vaden is going to be the preacher."

Papa would say, "Vaden is a good boy and someday he will make his mark, but God has His hand on this little stuttering, stammering child here." He would pull Oral over to him, pat him on the head and say, "This is the one."

Nobody believed Papa.

When Oral graduated from grade school to junior high he was elected king of the school. He was to be presented with the queen in the final assembly program at the end of the school term. When he went home and told Papa he had to have some new clothes, Papa just gave him that hungry preacher's look. Oral knew the offering that week was too small to buy new clothes.

So Oral got a job, selling newspapers after school and he sold enough to buy a completely new wardrobe: a ninety-eight-cent pair of tennis shoes, a sixty-nine-cent pair of overalls, and a forty-nine-cent shirt. On the morning of the assembly, he wore his new outfit.

The teacher took one look at him and said, "Oral, you had better run home and get dressed."

He said, "I am dressed."

Mary Lou White, daughter of a well-to-do family, had been elected queen. Oral didn't know how she would be dressed, but even if he had known, it wouldn't have mattered because he had on his best. When he got out in the hall and saw her dressed in a beautiful white satin evening gown it was one of the most embarrassing moments in his life.

But Oral gave her his arm, and they marched into the assembly room at the sound of the music. They were crowned and presented. After the queen made her bow, Oral made his. He was a king, even in denim overalls.

When Oral was fifteen, he felt he'd had enough. Enough ridicule about his inability to speak, enough belittling because he wasn't as outgoing as his brother Vaden, enough going to bed hungry, enough religion. He decided to leave home.

When he announced his intentions, Mama began to cry and Papa to exhort and threaten. "I'll put the police on your trail and they'll bring you back," Papa said.

Oral replied, "If you do, I'll just run away again."

Then they prayed. Mama said, "Oral, you will never be able to go farther than our prayers. We will pray and ask God to send you home, and He will."

Oral left Ada and went to Atoka, Oklahoma, where he found a place to live in a judge's home. The man gave him access to his law books and Oral began to study them fervently. He made up his mind to be a lawyer and someday governor of Oklahoma.

Meanwhile he had school and work. He got up at 4 A.M. to build the fires and do chores in the judge's home, carried a full load at school, practiced basketball with the team after school, and then went home to a paper route and to study until midnight. He wrote a column for the *Ada Evening News* and on Saturdays he worked in a

49

grocery store. Oral Roberts had left home to make something of himself and he worked hard at it. He was an A student and class president and a first-string basketball player. He did everything his heart desired but more than his body could stand.

One night during a basketball game, he collapsed on the floor, blood coming from his mouth. He lost consciousness briefly, and when he awoke he was in the back seat of his coach's car. "Oral, you're going home," he said.

The doctors came in to examine him and the verdict was not a pleasant one. Oral Roberts had tuberculosis in both lungs.

For 163 days, he lay in bed. He went from 160 to 120 pounds. Sweating at night, coughing blood, feverish, in constant pain. Unable to stand or walk. There were no miracle drugs then; no penicillin. Oral became discouraged and bitter. He cursed the day he was born.

One day his sister Jewel walked in and announced, "Oral, God is going to heal you." Something quickened inside him. There *was* hope. God knews where he was and He cared.

Soon after, Elmer, his eldest brother, borrowed a car and with his last thirty-five cents came to take Oral to a revival meeting. He had heard about an evangelist who prayed for the sick. He was convinced his little brother could be helped.

Elmer put a mattress in the back of the car and carried Oral out of the car and then into the meeting. Oral sat there in a rocking chair with pillows on both sides. When the evangelist finished preaching he came over and put both hands on Oral's head and prayed, "Thou foul disease! I command you in the name of Jesus to come out of this boy's lungs. Loose him and let him go."

The next thing, Oral was up from the rocker and running across the front shouting, "I'm healed! I'm healed!" Not only could he *breathe,* he could *talk.* He took deep breaths, going all the way to the bottom of his lungs without burning pain, coughing, or hemorrhaging. And then he took the microphone and walked up and down the platform, telling people plainly what Jesus of Nazareth had done for him.

When he went back to the clinic to have

his lungs fluoroscoped, the doctor said, "Son, forget you ever had TB. Your lungs are sound."

Within two months, that poor, sick, *healed* and *restored* runaway preached his first sermon. He and another young man held a service in the Homer schoolhouse. In the late afternoon, Oral went into the woods and preached to the trees. He found a Scripture in Mark, and as he preached the trees changed to people in his mind's eye. He practiced for over an hour and then went to the schoolhouse.

He preached to the people for twenty minutes and two of them gave their hearts to Jesus. It was a little sermon but it was a start. The two young evangelists stayed for two weeks, preaching every night and sometimes sleeping on the schoolhouse floor. At the end of the week, the church took an offering for them. Oral's half came to eighty-three cents.

Oral felt he had done his best and he was happy because he felt he was doing God's work. From then on he began to read his Bible more and pray at length. He went to camp meetings to seek more of God and the Holy Spirit, playing his guitar in little camp-meeting orchestras, ignoring adoring schoolteachers and everybody else. He continued to preach in little churches, bearing witness to God's healing power.

Finally, Oral Roberts began searching for a wife. Papa and Mama Roberts moved to Westville, where my parents lived, the year after I left for Texas.

Oral met my parents, and when they mentioned their daughter, Evelyn, he remembered the schoolteacher at the Sulphur camp meeting. Extremely practical Oral began to ask all over town, "Is Evelyn the type of girl I would want for my wife? Can she cook? What about her temper?" He even dated my sister to find out what I was like!

Two years overdue, in my thinking — but in God's *perfect* timing — Oral found me. Children of poor, deeply spiritual parents, drifting from God in our own ways, coming back to Him through loving grace, now preparing to unite our lives to each other and to a ministry — it was going to be Oral and Evelyn Roberts.

Miss Evelyn

If I had any time on my own as a little girl — when I didn't have to carry in wood or help my mother — you could have found me making a blackboard. I was fascinated with blackboards and the idea of using a blackboard to teach. If I couldn't find anything but a matchstick, I'd go outside and form a blackboard on the ground and write with that matchstick. And I was always giving someone an examination!

I wanted to be Miss Evelyn, the schoolteacher. I would have preferred that the Lord call me to be a missionary, but in case He didn't, I prepared myself to become a schoolteacher.

I used to love to get in bed with my grandparents early in the cool summer mornings or at night before I'd go to sleep. Grandmother would hold me in her arms and say, "Evelyn, you know what you want to be when you're grown, don't you?"

"Yes, a schoolteacher, Grandmother."

"All right, Evelyn, I want you to learn English. That's one thing you must always do — speak perfect English. Don't ever make mistakes in your grammar. You must talk all of your life, and you must learn to speak your words correctly if you are to be a schoolteacher. I don't want you ever to use slang. It's not ladylike, and it's not necessary. If you know the English language you never have to use slang."

I was a tiny girl but I never forgot her advice. Grandmother was always encouraging me to study. She'd say, "Evelyn, *make* something of yourself. Don't fool away your time. Use your time to good advantage. Study and make something of yourself. Get the best education you can get."

Grandmother set her sights very high for me and she made a great impression on me.

(The things Grandmother told me stayed strong in my mind when my own children were growing up. "Ain't" wasn't heard in our house — ever! Our children couldn't use poor grammar because I wouldn't tolerate it. Oral helped me with this. He could never stand to hear anybody mumble his words. If you ask our children they'll tell you, "Dad used to put us on his lap and say over and over, 'Don't mumble your words. If anything is worth saying, it's worth saying distinctly — *speak your words plainly.*' ")

Even before I graduated from high school, I passed the teacher's examination and received my teacher's certificate. Teachers with college degrees were scarce in those days and since I agreed to go on to college, I was allowed to begin teaching elementary grades right away.

I appreciated every hour of college I was able to earn because I worked hard for it. My parents had no money for college expenses, so I borrowed money from my grandfather for my first summer's work at Northeastern State Teacher's College in Oklahoma. Later he helped me borrow from a bank so I could attend classes at Texas College of Arts and Industries at Kingsville, Texas, near where he lived.

(Oral finished paying that debt to my grandfather after we were married and my grandfather's personal relationship with Jesus came largely because of that. He had never expected to see his money again after I married.)

While I was attending college in Kingsville, I lived in a boardinghouse with a girl named Dorothea. Dorothea's family had a little farm on Baffin Bay, right on the Gulf of Mexico, just about fifteen miles from Kingsville, and I often went to their home for weekends. The family was German, as my parents were, and I loved to be with them. One day I asked, "Dorothea, do you know of a school in this area that needs a teacher in September? I've just got to make some money."

"Well, my dad is on the school board but I don't know if there's an opening for a teacher. I'll ask him."

The next time Dorothea went home she talked to her father, and when she came back she said, "My dad wants you to come out." He wanted to hear me play the piano before he'd hire me. I played the piano for him and started teaching that September.

I moved out to Baffin Bay — but I continued my study at TCAI on Saturdays and in the summers, commuting to Kingsville about twenty miles away. We bought our groceries and went to church in Riviera, a little town about three miles from the bay. I shared a boardinghouse with the other two teachers; we lived practically on the beach. I'll never forget the red snapper fish we'd catch — the best you could get. We'd buy oysters sometimes and have beach parties.

The school was a consolidated type that served the entire country area. We taught the children until they finished the tenth grade and then they were bused into town for the eleventh and twelfth grades.

I taught third and fourth graders as my homeroom, and Spanish and math to junior high students.

I enjoyed teaching and at one time planned to make it my lifetime career. Looking back, I can see how the Lord used my training and experience for His glory. It was all in His plan.

In fact, it was my status as a teacher that impressed Oral more than anything else when he met me. A schoolteacher was something special in his eyes.

Because Oral had contracted tuberculosis he wasn't able to finish high school. One of the things he did before he started college was to order a correspondence course in English. Oral has always used good grammar but there were some things that caused him problems.

Even today, I'm baffled when highly educated people say "we" when they should say "us," or "sit" when it should be "sat," or "lie" when it should be "lay." That's always bothered me.

So I tried to help Oral with his grammar because I didn't want him to be embarrassed in public or when he was around educated people. The Lord helped me to help Oral in his study. The Lord also knew — although I didn't — that someday I would have to speak publicly. He knew my husband would speak to millions, and our children would make public witness for Him. He used my teaching experience to help them.

With my parents telling me to pray and to study the Bible and learn the Word of

God on one hand, and my grandmother stressing education and teaching on the other, I really couldn't have avoided either profession. Thirty years later, it seems quite right to me that I was a teacher who married a preacher. But in 1938, it was my teaching contract that almost upset my wedding.

Wedding Bells
and Christmas Bells

Oral proposed to me in September 1938 and then went back to his preaching obligations in Oklahoma. I went back to my third and fourth graders. Once again, we resumed our "mailbox" romance, exchanging letters every day.

Love by mail is better than no love at all, but it is a poor expression for young love. Soon, Oral began to write letters saying, "Evelyn, I love you and I need you. Please set the wedding date up from June to Christmas."

To have a Christmas wedding meant I would have to break my teaching contract. The school board had a fixed rule against hiring married teachers. When Oral's letters grew more persistent, I went to the school board and revealed my plans to marry. I didn't want to break the contract

I had signed but I wanted to please Oral; I could see no other way. But instead of asking me to resign, the school board said, "Go ahead and get married. You can teach for us as long as you want to. We like your teaching and when you do leave us, we'll give you a recommendation to teach anywhere you like." (When God is for you, who can be against you?)

With nothing else to hinder us, Christmas Day was set as our wedding day. We planned a church wedding — something the little church in Westville had never had. Reverend Oscar Moore performed the ceremony.

Christmas bells and wedding bells blended in beautiful harmony that wonderful day when I became Mrs. Oral Roberts. Oral's cousin, Lona Roberts, sang "I Love You Truly," and my sister Ruth was my bridesmaid. I walked down the aisle on one side of the church and Oral walked down the opposite side. We met at the altar where Reverend Moore was waiting with the Bible in his hand. Our wedding ceremony lasted only ten minutes but it brought us together for eternity.

"Forevermore," I whispered to myself as we left the church. *"Oral is mine and I am his."*

Oral had borrowed twenty dollars from the bank for our wedding and he gave Reverend Moore five dollars to perform the ceremony. Reverend Moore had driven one hundred miles so this pay was small. For several years after we were married, we sent the Moores a check at Christmas to make up for the poor pay at our wedding. One year Oral asked him, "Oscar, don't you think my debt should be paid by now?"

Oscar's reply was, "Oral, you can stop any time — whenever you think you've paid what she's worth."

Because I was still under my teaching contract I went back to Texas to teach after we were married. I spent much of the spring semester away from my husband. It was a lonely existence for both of us. We were apart during our courtship and then again during the first months of our marriage.

Oral's letters were my only strength. But one day I opened a letter that began,

"Dear Brother, In reply to your invitation to hold a meeting in your church. . . ." I blushed to think about the passionate love letter that some bewildered preacher had received. I knew Oral *really* missed me to get the two letters mixed!

At last my term was over and I boarded a bus to join Oral and become a full-time wife. I'll never forget what the bus driver said to me as he helped me load my trunk: "Well, Evelyn, you're going to be the wife of a preacher and all you'll ever have is a houseful of kids."

He didn't know Oral.

Preacher's Wife

I married Oral Roberts on December 25, 1938, because I loved him and for no other reason. I had never heard him preach and really had only my mother's word that he could.

After we had been married only a few days, we visited the church his parents pastored in Konawa, Oklahoma. Papa asked Oral to speak for him at the Wednesday night Prayer Meeting. Well — here was my big moment and I blew it. When Oral read his Scripture and then looked over at me, I had my head bowed praying for him.

He thought my head was bowed because I was ashamed of him and he was crushed. Later he said to me, "Well, I'm sorry I disappointed you."

"Honey, you didn't disappoint me. Your

sermon was beautiful. I was so proud of you, Oral.''

''Then why did you have your head down?''

''I was praying. Didn't you want me to pray for you?''

''From now on, pray before the service and hold your head up and look at me while I preach!''

Before we married, I asked Oral if he was one of those young preachers who believed in having a houseful of children. He said that he certainly wanted children, but he promised he wouldn't ask for more than two. He named them then and there: David and Rebecca. They came in reverse order, however (and I added Ann to the name Rebecca and Ronald to David). Life doesn't always work out as planned and our bonus babies were Richard and Roberta. We wouldn't change it for the world.

I became pregnant shortly after we were married and every place we went during that first fall of evangelistic work, the ladies of the church gave me a baby shower. When Rebecca was born, she had seventeen baby dresses. I shall never forget that. I had a layette that was almost unbelievable.

I went home to Oral's parents while they still lived in Konawa to have my baby. In fact, Rebecca was born in their front bedroom. December 16, 1939 — what a night to remember! Oral acted every bit the part of a typical father-to-be. The doctor came and sent him for a nurse who lived out in the country. The nurse later said the way Oral drove the car she didn't think she would ever get to her patient safely. Everything turned out all right though, and Rebecca Ann, a beautiful little girl, arrived on schedule. Oral acted as if no one had ever had a baby before. We couldn't imagine anyone having a baby as wonderful as ours. Rebecca had long, black hair and blue eyes — as blue as the sky. Everyone fell in love with her at first glance.

She was the last grandchild Mama Roberts was able to care for and she said many times, "I felt as though she was my very own." She would come early in the morning and get Rebecca out of her little bassinet and take her into the living room.

I could hear Papa and her chuckling and talking about how sweet and pretty Rebecca was. And, of course, church people came all day, every day, to see her.

Having a baby only added to the problems of our nomad existence while evangelizing. Most of the churches where we ministered were small and couldn't afford to house us in motels or hotels. So, bless the pastors and their wives, they had to host us. These experiences varied widely, from a gracious, hospitable welcome to a feeling that we were sleeping in their home only because the church couldn't afford anyplace else. Now, that surely made us feel great, especially when we knew we were scheduled to stay two or three weeks. We had to live in their homes, washing diapers and walking the floor with Rebecca during her crying, sleepless nights, and we were just as miserable as they were.

Every night I took my baby with me to the service, rain or shine, snow or sleet. (This was years before baby-sitters were known by that name.) I usually played the piano with Rebecca in her bassinet close enough so that when she was restless, I reached out with my left hand and shook the bassinet until she went to sleep.

We didn't know what a home of our own was like until Rebecca was two, when we went to Fuquay Springs, North Carolina, to pastor a church. A man who had accepted Jesus and had experienced the baptism in the Holy Spirit decided to build a church where the Bible would be emphasized. He constructed the building and then he asked us to come and fill it with a congregation.

(Even now after thirty-five years have passed I often say to Oral on a stormy night, "Oh, Honey, I do thank the Lord for a home like this where I can stay inside and not have to go out.")

I shall never forget trying to get Rebecca used to sleeping in her own bed, the first bed aside from ours she had ever had. She was so used to touching me that she refused to sleep unless she could reach out and hold my hand. Finally, Oral had enough of the hand holding. He thought I was spoiling her so he told her she must sleep by herself. I shall never forget how she sobbed in the darkness until (without Oral's knowing it) I stuck my foot out of the bed and across to her until she could reach my big toe. Clutching my toe in her hand, she went to sleep.

As a pastor, Oral made it a practice to visit the members of his church whether they called him or not. Some of them stood in awe of him at first, but he always broke down the barrier by raiding the refrigerator and asking if the lady of the house had any "beans, corn bread, and buttermilk."

Later, in the early days of the crusades, Oral sometimes accepted invitations to homes of friends for dinner. In one crusade, he mentioned in a sermon that he was very fond of corn bread and pinto beans. Without exception, everywhere we went for dinner in that town they served him corn bread and pinto beans. He decided to let well enough alone.

Oral was also a street preacher in those days. On Saturday afternoons, he would put a loudspeaker on top of his car, drive to a strategic street corner, park the car, and play records to attract attention. People were drawn by the music and they'd gather at the corner. Sometimes forty or fifty persons would gather, and then Oral would get out of the car and preach to them. The needs of people have always been his greatest concern and he felt he just had to reach the people who wouldn't come to church. The only way he knew was to preach to them on the streets. Often, I would be inside the car managing the music and loudspeaker and Rebecca, while he was preaching and talking to the people on the corner. Oral played the guitar and sometimes he and I would sing during those street meetings.

One Saturday we had a trio of girls with us. They had come to hold a special meeting in the church. Oral put these girls in the back seat of the car and we went up and down the streets of the town with the girls singing loudly over the car speaker from the back seat. The church filled with people who were hungry for the Lord.

Those may not have been very sophisticated times but they were good, happy times which the Lord used to further His Kingdom. We stayed in Fuquay Springs for a year and when we left nearly 350 persons were regularly attending the church.

The people in that North Carolina church were wonderful. They all had gardens and they brought me so many fresh vegetables and fruits that I was kept busy canning all summer. Oral's dad came to visit us and he helped me pick the vegetables and prepare them. Together, we picked bushels of produce and I canned over 300 quarts of fruits and vegetables. I didn't know I was pregnant at the time and due to the heat and exertion I lost what would have been our second baby.

In August we returned to Oklahoma. Our denomination assigned Oral to the pastorate of a church in Shawnee. We stayed there for three years and during that time, Ronald David was born. Ronnie was the sweetheart of all the church and they spoiled him right along with Rebecca. That's also when Oral began studying at Oklahoma Baptist University.

While we were in Shawnee, Oral started a drive for a small religious college in Oklahoma. He raised the first $1,000 in our church. Then he made a tour all through Kansas and Oklahoma and helped raise thousands of dollars to help establish the school. It was known as Southwestern College in Oklahoma City and it is still a growing educational center. Oral taught one semester in the college during the first year.

From Shawnee we went to Toccoa, Georgia, but we didn't stay long. To be honest, that was the one time I think we were out of God's perfect will. Not that we didn't do well there. People were blessed by Oral's ministry, but the Georgia Conference would not accept Oral as a member. The church people accepted him as their pastor and wanted him, but the denominational conference would not accept him because he was an out-of-state preacher. Unless one was a member of the conference of that state, one couldn't pastor a church. So even though Oral pleased the people, he could not stay. We returned to Shawnee and he reentered college at Oklahoma Baptist University.

We were really living by faith the year we moved back to Shawnee. The church we had pastored had another pastor by the time we came back. Oral preached on weekends in surrounding towns to support us and went to classes during the week.

I felt terrible because I was not working and helping out with expenses. We had two children and I felt they needed me at home, but I also felt I should do something to help pay the rent and grocery bills. We had sold our car, so when Oral had a preaching assignment he had to go to the edge of town and hitch a ride to where he was scheduled to minister. He did that for *two* semesters. One day he collapsed from exhaustion on the front steps of the college.

That's when I decided I just *had* to get a job. It was right after World War II and jobs were scarce. The only thing I was qualified to do was teach and to do that, I needed to go back to school and renew my teaching certificate. We didn't have the money for that so I went down to a five-and-dime store and got a job. It didn't pay very well. In fact, after I paid the baby-sitter each week, I came home with only fifteen dollars. I consoled myself by thinking that would at least help a little bit with the grocery bills.

When I left each morning to go to work, I put part of Oral's lunch in the refrigerator and part of it in the oven. I'd leave a little note on his plate saying, "Look in the refrigerator for your salad. Look in the oven for your hot food." I began coming home to find that the food had not been touched. I said, "Honey, weren't you hungry at noon?"

"No."

"Well, Oral, you *have* to eat to keep your strength."

"I wasn't hungry."

After several days of this, I sat down with him and said, "Oral, I want you to tell me *why* you aren't eating your lunch."

"Evelyn, *no* man wants to eat his lunch at home with his wife at work. I didn't want you to go to work. I don't want you to work now. You just believe with me and God will supply our needs."

That was my first and last employment outside my home except to help with Oral's work. His career became my career.

Soon after, we moved to Enid to pastor a church. Oral began classes at Phillips University. He was a very busy young man. Oral was always concerned about the Sunday school in the churches he pastored and he spent many hours devising ways to make them grow. His Sunday school departments were organized to perfection. Many people from other churches came to study his methods.

Oral especially loved the sick and they loved him. He visited them often and always had prayer for them. Many times they were healed.

I've always been a person who rolled with the punches. If Oral said "Move," I moved. If he said, "We're going to stay for a while," then I was content to stay. It was only when he was *deciding* whether to move or stay that I'd get upset. As long as he was content at a church, I'd invite the church members to our home and go visiting with him. I never missed a prayer meeting or a Sunday school class or a church service unless one of the children was sick. I enjoyed being a pastor's wife and seeing the people in our congregations grow in the knowledge of the Lord.

The fact that I married Oral Roberts didn't mean that he was at my beck and call. As long as Oral pastored churches, he made himself available to his parishioners day and night. I was first in his heart all right, but the needs of the people seemed to have first *call* on his services.

I have always enjoyed digging in the earth, planting flowers and vegetables and watching them grow. When I gather in the vegetables, I feel that I have accomplished something. Oral used to help me in the garden when he had time, but he was usually too busy ministering to people.

One day, the potatoes I had planted were ready to dig and I asked Oral if he would help me. He was quick to say yes and he planned to take off the whole afternoon for the job. He put on some old clothes and off we went to the garden.

He had dug only two or three mounds of potatoes when the telephone rang. Someone was at the point of death and they wanted "Brother Roberts" to come and pray. Of course, Oral hurriedly changed clothes and went as fast as he could to pray for the person. I stayed in the garden, digging potatoes alone.

Soon Oral came back, changed into his old clothes, and dug a few more potatoes. Again the telephone rang. This time someone who needed an emergency appendectomy couldn't afford an ambulance and wanted the pastor to drive him to the hospital. Oral went.

Back in the garden once more, I just knew that we would finish without any more interruptions. I was wrong. Oral had dug only a few more potatoes when the familiar ring summoned him again. I'll never forget the look on Oral's face. Exasperated, he threw down the spade and said, "I'll never dig another potato as long as I live." You're right! He has kept *that* vow!

But the *real* reason Oral has shunned digging potatoes has not been simply because he no longer wanted to help me. It has been a deeper reason, a reason which drastically altered my life after nearly eight years of being "the preacher's wife."

The Crisis of 1947

When Oral proposed to me, he didn't mention his call to the healing ministry. He knew that God had spoken to him in a definite way, but he had never told me about it. When we were pastoring in Enid, God began dealing with him in a new way.

In his dreams at night, Oral began to see the human race — lost, sick, afraid, frustrated, tormented, oppressed. He heard its screams of fear and misery, its sobs, its wails of frustrations. What he saw and heard and felt tore him to pieces inside.

One day his sociology professor declared in class that it was scientifically impossible for a woman to have been made from a man's rib as the Bible declares. Oral was sitting in the back row, waiting for someone to challenge the statement. Nobody did. He heard God's voice again speak to him:

Son, don't be like other men. Don't be like other preachers. Be like My Son Jesus and heal the people as He healed them.

God also showed him there was only one source of original information about Jesus, life, and ministry, and that was in the four Gospels and the Book of Acts in the New Testament. He felt compelled to read through those five books consecutively, three times during the next month. He'd get down on his knees and read for a long time each day, in addition to his church work and college studies. Many times I'd find his eyes filled with tears. Oral wanted so much to preach the gospel, heal the sick, and emphasize the working power of faith, but he didn't know where to begin. A desire to be more like Jesus burned in his soul.

I began waking in the night to find him walking the floor, or kneeling in front of the little gas stove praying. I knew he was troubled. I'd ask, "Oral, Honey, what's wrong with you? Are you sick?"

"No."

"Well, what's wrong?"

"I'm just praying, Evelyn."

So I'd go back to bed. I figured if he wanted to pray in the middle of the night, that was his privilege and I wouldn't disturb him. It kept on though until one night I was awakened by Oral's sobbing and praying in his sleep in the corner of the bathroom. He was on his knees by the little furnace. As he looked up to see me standing there, I touched his shoulder and said, "Oral, what in the world are you doing?"

"Evelyn, I don't know."

I led him back into the bedroom where we sat down on the side of the bed.

"Oral, what's the matter with you?"

"I don't know."

"Yes, you do, Oral."

He looked at me as if a sudden realization had hit him. "Yes, Evelyn, I *do* know what is wrong with me. I haven't known until this minute, but now I know. My time to heal the sick is come and I don't have the power of God to do that."

Then he told me how the Lord had

spoken to him twelve years before when his brother was taking him to the revival service where he was healed of tuberculosis. He told me how God said: "Son, I am going to heal you, and you are to take My healing power to your generation." He had never told another person what he shared with me that night.

Well, mercy. When he told me, I realized why the struggle had been so great. He had known all those years what God wanted him to do, but he didn't know when or how. He felt the time had come to start a ministry that emphasized healing and he wanted to do it under God's direction.

He had the worry, too, of knowing that if he gave up his church, he would have a wife and two children to support without a salary. It's difficult for anybody to give up a regular salary and say, "I'll trust the Lord all the way." If you have never done this, you don't know how hard it is.

But Oral said, "I'm not afraid, Evelyn. I just want to be sure I'm doing it the *Lord's* way. I don't know what to do."

"Oral, if God is telling you to do something, He will also show you the *way* to do it. You do know what to do."

"Yes, I do," he said, "Don't cook for me any more until I tell you."

I believed, with Oral, that fasting and prayer would show him the direction to take. I didn't say to Oral, "You fast." I don't think any person has the right to tell another person how to run his spiritual life. And I don't think that because Jesus fasted forty days and nights means any of us can or should. I think people get hung up on things like this in the Bible. Unless the Lord tells a person to fast and pray about something with which he's struggling, I don't think a fast is going to do him any good.

Recently, a woman told me she was fasting for forty days. I said to her, "Let me tell you something. Jesus is the only One that I know Who could do without food for that long. You are only a human being. Don't think you can do what Jesus did."

I asked her, "Are you praying for something definite to happen?"

She said, "Yes."

"All right, then, as soon as that happens,

or you have the inner knowing that it will happen, give up your fasting. What is fasting for? It's to reach a place of answers to prayers." Jesus wasn't told to fast for forty days. He fasted for an *answer* to His prayers and when the answer came, He quit fasting.

So Oral didn't fast any definite number of days. He would come in after fasting a day or two and say, "I think I should eat dinner now." I'd fix something for him. I didn't question him. I cooked for him when he asked and I didn't cook for him *until* he asked.

The day he had his answer, I knew it. He parked the car and ran up on the porch. When he opened the front door, I knew immediately he'd heard from the Lord. By the way he ran, by the way he opened the door, by the way he looked — he was a different person. He shouted, "Evelyn, cook me a meal."

"What *happened,* Oral?"

"I've heard from the Lord."

"Fine." I didn't ask him immediately what the Lord had said, but later he told me what had happened.

Oral had gone to his office at the church that day and locked all the doors so he wouldn't be disturbed. He lay on the floor and said, "Lord, I make a vow to You right now that I won't get up until You answer me. I've fasted all these days and I have prayed. I have sought Your will. I've done everything I know to do. Now I've got to have an answer today." He lay on the floor all day, praying.

Late in the afternoon he heard the Lord say, *"Stand on your feet."*

"Well," Oral told me, "I didn't think the Lord would speak to me or anybody like *that*. I'd been lying on the carpet so long it was hard to get up, but I stood there until I heard the next words, *'Go get in your car. Drive two blocks and turn right.'*" When Oral had driven two blocks and turned right, the Lord spoke a third time and said, *"From this moment, you will feel My power in your right hand."*

Oral is a practical person and Christianity is very practical to him. Oral says, "The Lord is a sensible Being and He talks to you on your sense level." God knew Oral would take orders in the same manner he likes to give orders, and He knew Oral would do exactly what He said to do.

A few days later, we called several of our close friends from the church. They came to our home and Oral shared with them what the Lord had told him. A couple of people encouraged him and gave their moral support, but some others discouraged him. Some said, "You'd better be careful, Brother Roberts. We accepted you as our pastor for at least seven years and you've only been here one year. You'd better be sure God is talking to you, because if you leave here before your seven years are over. . . ."

Oral always checks the things he feels the Lord tells him to do with what is written in the Bible. The Bible says to "test the Spirits" (I John 4:1) to see if what is said agrees with the Bible. So he said to some of the men in the church, "I want to have a few meetings in this area on the nights we don't have meetings at our church. Let's call the pastors of churches in other towns and tell them we want to come and share with their congregations and minister to them." That's exactly what they did and as they preached and prayed, the people were blessed and healed.

It had been almost fifty years since many of these ministers had seen God's healing power at work in their congregations. It was new to most of the church people, too. People became more and more interested in the healing ministry.

Then we began holding prayer meetings in our church — praying for the Spirit to move and for people to be healed. On Sunday afternoons, we held special services that emphasized healing. People would fill the church and we'd have to put in extra seats. The Lord marvelously healed people. But, all the time, some stood back, watching and wondering if it was really *God* at work. They watched Oral like hawks. Some were against him and some for him. Some thought he was in God's will, some thought he wasn't.

We started a radio broadcast from our church and soon the program took more money to produce than our church alone could give. Oral began telling people over the radio, "Our broadcast will be beamed out to you only if you're interested in hearing it. I'm going to send you a little yellow pledge envelope and if you'd like to have a part in keeping this radio program on the air, return your envelope to us and we will use every dollar for the radio ministry."

The people responded and Oral did what he had promised. He turned all the envelopes over to a committee in the church and they counted the money and paid for the radio programs.

One man was impressed, though, by the *amount* of money that came in — and not with the more important fact that the Lord was meeting the need.

A traveling evangelist had come to town, too, and had made his offering pleas sound almost like a public auction. This man had gone to those services and he thought he saw a good thing for himself with Oral. He came to Oral and said, "I can see this is a money racket and I want in on it."

Talk about being hurt! I don't think Oral has ever been hurt more than he was that day. He came home as white as a sheet. I'll never forget the way he looked when he walked in the front door. He said,

"Evelyn, I'm not going to go into the healing ministry."

"You're what?"

"I'm not going into the healing ministry." And then he told me what this man had said. "If people think I'm out for the money, I'm quitting right now."

I said, "Oral, can't you see through this? Can't you see that this is the devil's trick to stop you? Money is the first thing he'll use against you. Probably many people will say what this man said. The devil must know you are going to do a great work for Him or he wouldn't be attacking you so. You're going to have to rebuke this and get this man and what he said out of your mind."

Oral prayed, "Lord, I want You to convince this man that he is wrong, and not release him from this feeling until he knows the truth." Months later, during an altar service, this man came up to Oral, crying so hard he could barely stand. "Oral," he said, "you've got to forgive me. I've been bound in my Spirit so that I'm no longer free. I apologize to you. I was wrong. God has got to forgive me, and you've got to forgive me so I can have peace in my heart again." And Oral prayed with him, and their friendship was restored.

Then Oral made a bold announcement. He planned a mass service in Enid and he vowed that this was the point of decision. Either God would have a thousand people present, meet all financial obligations of the meeting without embarrassing pleas, and heal people or Oral would quit the ministry and accept a job as a salesman in a clothing store! I still shudder when I think about that vow. It was a desperate and irrational thing to do, but the struggle in Oral's heart had reached such proportions he was a desperate man. He wanted a definite, conclusive decision. Would God honor his faith, or not? He has certainly never recommended that other people do what he did.

We held the meeting on Sunday at two o'clock in the Educational Building in the center of town. Oral preached a sermon entitled, "If You Need Healing — Do These Things." Some 1,200 persons attended. When the offering was quietly taken to meet expenses, the ushers found they had $3.03 above the cost for renting the building. About halfway through the sermon the power of God seemed to consume Oral and he began to pray for the sick who were there. A woman who had suffered a stiff arm for more than thirty-eight years was wonderfully healed. Oral prayed for people until six o'clock and many left the service healed in their bodies and blessed in their souls. Our home town — the hardest place of all — and God had worked miracles.

Our healing ministry was launched. God had confirmed the call and this was *how* He wanted it done.

We prayed together, "Lord, *where* do You want us to go from here? We know we must give up pastoring churches and we know You want us in the evangelistic field, but where shall we go?"

We knew Oral would have to fly a great deal in order to spend most of his time preaching rather than traveling and still have time for his family. Tulsa was central in the United States and had good plane connections. It seemed the logical place for us to go. We drove to Tulsa to see the city and we decided to settle there. This was in the year 1947.

In that same year, a Tulsa pastor had erected a large tent on Main Street, intending to hold a continuous revival throughout the summer. He asked Oral to preach one Tuesday night. It was unseasonably cold and rainy and only about 200 attended. However, many people accepted Christ and several were miraculously healed. The pastor asked Oral to stay and preach, which he did for nine weeks.

One night during this revival, an enraged bystander fired a revolver at Oral as he was preaching. The bullet tore through the canvas just two feet above Oral's head. The story of this attempt on his life was carried by the media nationwide, and it focused the attention of thousands on what God was doing on North Main Street in Tulsa, Oklahoma in the summer of 1947.

In just a few short, turbulent, decisive months, Oral had entered a new ministry that had gained national recognition.

With this new ministry came a new life for me. I knew Oral would be away from home for long periods of time and I didn't know how the children and I were going to stand it.

The financial uncertainty didn't worry me. We had started our marriage with borrowed money and had never been wealthy. Oral had always managed to make a living, providing us with enough to eat and to wear.

My concern was being separated from Oral, the man I had married and wanted to be with for the rest of my life. It was a crisis time for me but in a different way.

I'll never forget the morning I drove from Enid to Tulsa to see Oral off on the plane to his first evangelistic crusade in the East. Neither of us had ever flown before.

He kissed me good-bye, walked up the steps, and disappeared inside. Tears came to my eyes as I thought: Yes, good-bye, Oral. I'll probably be doing this the rest of my life. While we are both young, we should be together, but we have to be apart.

Reaching Out to the World

When Oral was in Victoria Falls, Rhodesia, he wrote in one of his letters to me:

Yesterday a native kept following me until I turned around and asked him what he wanted.

"You are Brother Oral Roberts, aren't you?"

"Yes, I am. How did you know who I am?"

"I saw you in the film. I know you."

Evelyn, missionaries have shown our film, *Venture into Faith,* in this area and this man has been converted to Christ and feels he knows me personally. I was amazed but Brother Freeman (the missionary with me) understood completely. He said,

"Oral, I once walked into a small hut in a little village out in the bush country, and your picture was hanging on the wall."

Oral finished his letter:

It's hard to explain why the Lord would use me to move this dark continent to Him. But I am willing.

Willing. I think that's the number-one key in explaining Oral's impact on this world. God has used him in the remote areas of faraway countries and He has used him in big, well-known cities because he has been *willing* to go wherever God asked him to go and do whatever God has asked him to do. If God told Oral today to move from Tulsa and go preach to natives in an uncharted jungle halfway around the world, you'd find him there as soon as he could get there, not because he likes the heat or discomfort or the travel and adventure, but because he wants to and is *willing* to obey God.

Certainly, we never envisioned the *extent*

of our ministry when we began in 1947. It has been a year-at-a-time growing process — in our hearts and in the hearts of millions of our partners.

During the first months in 1947, Oral conducted his crusade meetings in large churches and in city auditoriums. The meetings were sponsored by local churches. To an extent, this created friction among churches in the cities where we ministered and Oral felt limited by denominational ties and the size of many church auditoriums. He made two decisions: to hold his meetings in a large "canvas cathedral tent," which would be a neutral place of worship for large crowds, *and* to hold *city-wide* meetings sponsored by *groups* of churches. He wanted to get the emphasis off denominations and put it on Jesus Christ. Of course, many of the people who attended our meetings later joined churches in their cities, but sponsoring church membership drives was not our purpose.

Oral took a step by faith and borrowed $9,000 toward the purchase of that first tent. I remember seeing it stretched out —

90 by 210 feet. It seemed so big to me I wondered if we would ever fill it to capacity.

Our first crusade with the tent was in Durham, North Carolina. The tent seated 3,000, and the first night we had 700. Three weeks later, the crowd exceeded 9,000 people! They filled that tent to capacity and completely surrounded it, standing ten deep all the way around the outside of the tent. We just couldn't believe that there were that many people who were really hungry for the Lord.

We were not total strangers to Durham because we had lived in North Carolina before, and many of those who came the first night were our friends. When they came and found the Lord was moving people's hearts and healing their bodies, the word spread quickly and people came from everywhere. It was a thrilling sight to me.

From Durham on, the meetings continued to grow. Attendance increased everywhere we went and soon we had to buy a larger tent. The second tent seated closer to 7,000 persons and during its second week of use, people were coming two hours before the meeting just to get a seat.

We always went to the tent meetings after the crowd was there, the singing was over, and the announcements had been made.

One of the church leaders or Bob DeWeese, our associate evangelist, would lead the congregation in singing, but for many years we had no special music. The people didn't want anything except to see Oral walk out on that platform. They came to hear him, and anything else just took up time until he got there.

We always offered the people a book of some kind during the meeting because we felt a book was something they could take home with them and read and receive help from long after we were gone. For many years we gave away Oral's book, *If You Need Healing, Do These Things*. We felt this was the most effective book people could have besides their Bible.

Oral came to the tent's platform, ready to preach — with a burning message in his heart not quenched by announcements — and preach he did, sometimes for more than two hours. Then, after he had finished his sermon, he would issue an invitation to people to come forward to accept Jesus Christ as their Lord and Savior. Over the years, people not familiar with our ministry have emphasized the healing lines of our crusades more than these invitations to accept Christ. They forget about the thousands who came forward seeking Jesus. Almost always, the numbers seeking Christ in salvation exceeded the number seeking prayers for healing.

After the altar call, and *only* after the altar call, the people would form a healing line — coming for individual prayer as Oral sat on a chair on the platform.

We had a healing line in the very first tent crusade, and people left their crutches, their hearing aids, their braces — everything you can imagine — behind in that tent. Our workers gathered up the debris. People left their sicknesses there and didn't want anything to remind them. Hundreds were miraculously healed by God. Many times, the services lasted from three to four hours because of the length of the healing line. The people would not be turned away from prayer.

We didn't put on a show for these people — we had no choir, no special programs, no lengthy appeals. But God put on a show — a miraculous display of His power and love — and this is what the people came for. I saw more than 12,000 people wade in the mud in Fayetteville, North Carolina. They sat in a rainstorm and it rained and rained. Before Oral began preaching, he asked the people to go home, but they wouldn't move. They preferred to sit in the mud. The men rolled up their trouser legs, took off their shoes, and Oral stood on the platform and preached.

I've seen people come and wrap themselves in blankets when the weather would turn cold. They were so hungry for the Gospel. People would walk through acres of parking lots, sit and stand through hot weather, cold weather, rain, storms — it didn't make any difference.

We bought several tents over the years — but never one large enough. The last tent we had seated 12,000 people, and many times I saw people stand eight and ten deep around the outside in the hot sun or rain.

One night I overheard a man say after a meeting, "I sure had a good place to *stand!*"

Sometimes, funny things happened. I always brought a small quilt to spread right by my seat in the early days so Richard and Roberta could go to sleep if they wanted to. And I'd always have the ushers save a seat for me at the end of an aisle so I could put the quilt down just inside. After all, these crusades were an every-night occurrence for us. I didn't miss a night and I wouldn't have for anything.

One night a woman began running around the tent, creating quite a disturbance, and soon she came over to where I was. She didn't know me, but she sat down on my lap and said loudly, "Well, here's a nice soft seat." Right there on my lap! We have laughed many times about that. The usher finally came and took her to her seat.

And sometimes not-so-funny things happened. During a crusade in Amarillo, Texas, a tornadolike wind struck our tent. While Oral was praying for the sick, lightning struck nearby and the lights went out. As the big tent began to fill with wind, it began to rise. The giant aluminum poles that held the canvas fell toward the people, but gently. The tent floated down on all of us. I carried Richard in my arms to the platform and huddled under it. People began to crawl from under the tent. Slipping through the hail and mud outside, they found their cars. Oral went from group to group, praying with them and praising God for their safety. Police and firemen came to assist. Oral eventually found us, safe but wet, and we went back to the hotel. We changed into dry clothes and huddled there, listening to radio reports. At 4 A.M. it was announced that no one had been killed and we went to bed.

The next morning Oral went to the hospital to pray for the injured, but only two of the 7,000 people who had attended had been kept at the hospital and they were not seriously injured. The blazing headline on the morning paper read: ESCAPE OF 7,000 CALLED A MIRACLE. And we agreed. We went to the crusade site that afternoon and again praised God. Chairs were twisted, the tent was in shreds, the lights were destroyed. But these things could be replaced. And soon they were.

In those days it was against the law in many of the southern states for Black people to sit with white people. Black people have always loved our ministry and attended the crusades, and it hurt us to see them put in a section to themselves, but the law said it had to be done that way and we couldn't change it. As a rule, held no meetings on Monday nights, but one week Oral announced, "Monday we are going to have a meeting for the Blacks here in this city. No white persons will be allowed. We want all our Black friends to come." Oral felt if he couldn't change the law he could at least reverse the process, and he did.

When we got to that meeting, the place was jammed with Black people. Every seat was filled and they were standing all around. About 10,000 were present.

You talk about getting rid of crutches and braces! I shall never forget one little woman on crutches. Oral prayed for her and she walked away with her crutches just as she had come. She got five or six steps away and Oral said to the audience, "She doesn't even realize what has happened to her. Somebody stop her."

One of the men stopped her and said, "Brother Roberts would like to talk to you." She turned around and looked at him.

Oral said, "Sister, aren't you being healed?" She just turned around again with her crutches and started off.

Again Oral said, "Sister, the Lord is trying to heal you." She turned around a second time and looked at him. A stunned expression came over her face and suddenly she *threw* down those crutches, and she went running through that audience. And I tell you, that crowd really came alive. Thousands were healed because of the inspiration they received from that one healing.

The tent crusades were an exciting time for me. I had never before witnessed so many people accepting Christ. It was unheard of in that time to have 500 or 1,000 people a night accept Jesus Christ. It just didn't happen in the churches.

Many church people were suspicious of us and what we were doing. People with needs never were. But the church people would say, "I wonder if it's of God, or is it of the devil?" It always seemed to be the church people who questioned. It didn't bother Oral. He just went ahead and preached regardless of race, creed, or denomination.

Many times I've heard him say, "When I preach to an audience or lay hands upon the sick, I can think of them in no other way than as God's people. I am unable in my spirit to put labels on them or prefer one over another."

Oral seems to know the Lord better than he knows me. He is more at home in the pulpit than he is in his own backyard.

I remember when Herb Lightman, the man who produced *Venture into Faith,* said to Oral, "You boggle me. When I talk to you in your room or somewhere else you are so ordinary. Even your speech is ordinary. When you are in the pulpit something comes upon you and you become another man. Your voice becomes vibrant. Every word you speak has great power and you do something to me."

I have often tried to capture in words that quality in Oral, and the spirit of the crusades, but I think a man who attended one of our crusades in the east said it best. He wrote:

The Oral Roberts sermons are actually the highlight of the meeting so far as I am concerned. I have been listening to sermons ever since I was a little boy. I have appreciated good sermons all my life. I enjoy a good sermon more than a good song. But with all that appreciation for great sermons, Oral Roberts is the only man on top of the earth who has ever held my attention for two hours and fifteen minutes and then closed, leaving me wishing that he would go on! Why? You tell me!

His Scripture lessons are unusually long for an evangelist. No snappy sentence texts are used to catapult his sermons into a sensational, disjointed appeal to men's ignorance of the Scriptures. Form the word go, he is a Bible preacher. The beginning of his message is deliberate, sometimes almost slow. Here again, I have wondered how he holds the people through those introductions. He never talks above their heads. He talks to their eyes. He probes their hearts. He never leaves them for a somersault on the Milky Way. He is always down-to-earth. He never teases them with so-called double talk. They understand his language. He never bores them with theological hairsplitting. With him, salvation is being saved. Healing is being healed. Holiness is getting right and living right. Jesus is the Savior of the world. Our God is a good God, and the devil is a bad devil.

His critics accuse him of being top-heavy on the healing idea. What the man preaches is faith in God. He preaches the Book of Acts and the four Gospels. The four Gospels tell what Jesus began to do and to teach. The Book of Acts tells how the disciples followed up His work after His death, resurrection, and ascension. And this is the source of most of the Oral Roberts sermons.

His style of preaching is pointed and positive. Only a minimum of time is spent preaching against things. He preaches for something. With a man-size microphone in his hands, he walks over the platform, his eyes sweeping every angle, every square foot of the great tent. There is hardly a person there but who feels he has been preached to before the sermon is over.

Oral Roberts's voice is pleasant to listen to. It never takes the tone of harshness. Even when he raises it sharply, it attracts rather than repels. Now his voice warns, now it cajoles, now it entreats, now it reaches out and seems to whip above the heads of the audience. But even the lash never quite descends to cut the people. Like the lash of a whip in the hands of an expert driver, it doesn't hurt the team; it merely spurs them to action.

His sermons are not sensational, but they are dramatic. He can assemble a group of people on the platform, put them through the paces of conversation and action, and make them see the thing he is talking about. His dramatic description of the dice game at the foot of the cross of Christ is an example of this. There is no cross there; there are no gambling soldiers there. And yet you see them all. Oral Roberts becomes the cross, the gamblers, the conversation. The characters come to life and you see them clearly. He rarely uses descriptive phrases, and yet he makes you see. His words are words of action.

Many times Oral and I have prayed together before a crusade. Whether I was in the room or not, if Oral became absorbed in the Spirit of God while praying, he forgot I was around and began to talk to the Lord as if He saw Him standing there. I have heard him ask the Lord to open his mind and help him give the deep truths of the Bible to the people in plain, simple language so they could understand.

I think that must be one of the reasons I have never tired of hearing my husband preach. If he were an "ordinary" preacher I would. But he speaks in ordinary language and that makes him an unusual preacher!

Too, Oral may have used the same subject a hundred times, but he always presents a new idea I've never heard before.

Occasionally, he'll turn to me and say,

"That's hot off the wire; I've never said that before." Which is the truth. And this is what I keep looking for and keep waiting for in his sermons — knowing that the Lord is going to reveal something new to him.

Some people think the day of revelation is absolutely over. They believe God revealed everything in the Bible and He's not going to reveal anything else. I agree that all God reveals to people now must agree with the Bible, but I don't believe the day of revelation is over. The Lord is still talking to people and giving people new thoughts.

When Oral prays over his sermons, the Lord opens up his mind and it begins to blossom. New thoughts come pouring in — new ideas being created through the power of the Holy Spirit.

I have often told Oral, "Honey, I don't know you when you're in the pulpit because you are a different personality." I've seen him at times so anointed by God that he wouldn't be able to recognize me in the congregation — and I don't recognize him as my husband. He seems like a new man to me.

Oral incorporated his ministry as early as 1948. We withdrew the several hundred dollars we had in our savings account — the first savings account we had ever had — and gave it to his attorneys to establish the Oral Roberts Association.

With experts in the field of business to handle affairs of the Association, Oral was relieved of having to think about money, and all his efforts went toward his ministry. He was constantly coming up with new projects to meet the needs of people.

In 1952 we filmed *Venture into Faith,* capturing for tens of thousands the spiritual blessing of a crusade. As our associates traveled across the United States and overseas to Africa and the Philippines showing this film, thousands of men and women were saved and healed. In just a month's showing behind the Iron Curtain, 6,000 people accepted Christ. Altogether, more than 250,000 people came to know Christ as their Savior through that film.

In 1953 we closed a crusade in southern California, and Oral headed for the next meeting, which was in the Northwest. He said, "Ride with me in the car, Evelyn, to Portland. Then I'll put you on the plane to go home and be with the children and I'll drive to Spokane." We had a lovely time driving up the coast of California and I hated to leave him and come home. But I am sure it was all in God's will.

Oral told me later, "As I was driving along from Portland to Spokane, the grain was waving in the wind and the sun, and there were big combines and machinery out in the fields separating the grain from the chaff. God spoke to me out of it and said, *'Whatever you can conceive, you can do.'*"

From that experience, Oral began a master plan to win a million souls for the Lord. A million decisions were recorded in less than three years as we traveled in World Outreach Crusades, including the Far East.

Through the 1950s and early 1960s we had four million-soul campaigns. During that time we traveled to South Africa — where we ministered to both Blacks and whites, and to lepers — and to Rhodesia, Australia, France, Holland, New Zealand, India, the Philippines, and other countries.

We began a television program and continued large crusade meetings across America.

A close friend once said to us, "Oral Roberts lives in a miracle on the edge of expectancy." That sense of expectancy has driven him around the world.

In 1973 Oral was inducted into the Oklahoma Hall of Fame, partly for putting Oklahoma on the world map. (I couldn't think of anybody more deserving!)

People all over the world know about Oklahoma because of him. A friend told me recently that when her mother was in Switzerland, she went into a camera shop to buy film and started talking to a tourist from South Africa who was also a visitor there. The South African lady asked, "Where are you from?"

"I'm from Tulsa, Oklahoma."

"Oh, that's where Oral Roberts lives. Do you know him?"

"Well, I don't know him personally, but my daughter and her husband know Oral and Evelyn very well."

"I would give anything to get one of his books. I've heard so much about them, but

I don't know how to get one."

This lady promised to send her one and did. Imagine — a Tulsan and a South African meeting in Switzerland to discuss Oral Roberts's ministry and the goodness of God!

Only because Oral Roberts was *willing* to accept a call.

Travels for Jesus

My role as wife to a world missionary has been thrilling. Walking over the rocky hillside where the Master's feet had walked made Jesus more real to me. There in the Holy Land — the Garden of Gethsemane where He prayed, up Golgotha's hillside where He died, by the Sea of Galilee where He calmed life's storms, in the city where He healed all that came unto Him, into the empty tomb from which He arose victorious — I walked in His steps and learned to love my Savior more than ever before. From early childhood I have longed to touch foreign soil in the name of Jesus. That desire seemed wonderfully fulfilled in Israel.

When we lived in Arkansas, I begged the Lord to call me to be a missionary. I wanted to be a missionary so strongly.

Missionaries would come to speak to us at school and church and they'd bring their little treasures and slides from foreign countries to show us what the Lord was doing. They'd give tremendous testimonies about what the Lord was doing for foreign peoples and I'd sit in the front pew, transfixed as they talked about taking the Good News of Jesus to the heathens. I yearned to go. I pleaded, "Lord, *please* call me."

I was taught that unless you had a *definite* call to do a special work, you dare not go. It was dangerous to travel in those days. And you didn't go alone, even if you were called. The denominations sent out couples or two women together. I was so jealous of my older girl friends who had received calls to be missionaries. I would see some of them cry because God called them to go far away from home and I would say to God, "Oh, please call *me*. I won't mind going so far."

From the age of twelve, I asked the Lord to call me, but He never did. I graduated from high school a few years later and took teacher's training courses.

I recently came across a letter to our children which showed how excited I was during that first trip to Israel:

My dear children,

I have seen things today that I never expected to see in my lifetime. In fact, I have to pinch myself to see if I'm really here. Everything is so ancient one could easily think he was living in Jesus' day.

This morning, I went with Daddy and the crew to film the Christmas story. They began outside in the shepherds' fields, where they graze their herds — near Bethlehem — in those same fields David watched over his sheep when he was a boy. The cool, crisp air in the shepherds' fields is breathtaking. The are no noises of industry — just the sound of a shepherd's horn or the passing of feet on the road.

Jericho is in a beautiful, tropical valley. They grow oranges, grapefruits, bananas, and dates. Everything is green and pretty. We passed by a well called Elisha's Well, or Fountain, and coming down the road was a group of women with pitchers on their heads just like in Bible days. It really thrilled me to see them.

This land where Jesus walked and talked gives me a feeling of peace I have never experienced before. It is indescribable. I feel Jesus so near me.

At night when I leave the hotel for a breath of air and I look over the old city of Jerusalem, even the quietness of the night and the closeness of the heavens seem to bring Jesus down to my fingertips. He must be hovering over this city. Even though it broke His heart and He wept over it — no doubt many times — I'm sure He must love it still as He did then.

Roberta Jean and Richard, I wish I had a kiss this morning from you. You are both so sweet. I'm so thankful you have plenty to eat and good clothes to wear. So many of these poor, little children over here have nothing. They never had a toy in their lives. They have no tricycles and no dolls. Some of them don't even have enough food to eat. They follow us around asking for money. Ronnie, many of the boys your size are shepherd boys. They stay out all day with a herd of sheep and goats. Sometimes they have a bite of lunch and sometimes they don't. We must be thankful to God for the food, clothes, and home we have. Jesus is so good to us. Being here where He lived and was crucified makes me love Him so very much.

All of you be sweet and don't forget to pray for us every day. Rebecca, I'm thinking about you tonight.

Daddy and I love every one of you the same. You are the most precious things we have in the world.

Love,
Mother

Christmas has had a new sacredness for me since the one I spent in Jerusalem and Bethlehem. The land where Jesus walked and talked gave me an indescribable feeling of peace. Although it was Christmas, quiet and peace were everywhere, no hustle and bustle and merrymaking as we see here.

On Christmas Eve the bells pealed out from the Church of the Nativity while Oral and I talked to a man from Romania and told him how Jesus could bring peace to his heart.

One morning I visited the upper room known as the Room of the Last Supper. It was the highlight of my visit to Israel. That room means many things to many people. But to me the greatest thing that happened in that room was the outpouring of the Holy Spirit on the day of Pentecost. Tradition also says that it was here that Jesus sat and washed His disciples' feet.

As I knelt and prayed, tears poured down my cheeks. I thought of how privileged I was to kneel where such profound events had happened. In my mind's eye I could see the 120 sitting around on the floor or on cushions when the Holy Spirit came with the sound of a rushing, mighty wind and sat upon each of them. I could see them with their boldness — with so much power that they rushed out of that room into the streets of the old city of Jerusalem and began to witness to whomever they met. The Holy Spirit was so strong upon them that crowds began to gather. They were so happy they wanted to tell the whole world and 3,000 were converted to Christ on that day.

As we finished praying, a man entered the room with a camera. He was a tourist from New Jersey. I asked him if he knew what happened in this room. But he knew only that the Last Supper took place here. He didn't know about the outpouring of the Holy Spirit at Pentecost. So we witnessed to him about what Jesus did and could do.

I came home from Israel with a new understanding of and burden for the Jewish people and the thousands of Arab refugees — so precious to God — whom we saw in camps there. Both Jews and Arabs seemed to have a good feeling for my husband and gave him many courtesies, as well as welcoming his prayers on their behalf.

As our ministry grew, we usually had an overseas crusade during the winter of each year. While it was cold here in the States, we'd go to someplace in the southern hemisphere where the summer weather was better for outdoor meetings. We generally had meetings in large stadiums and always by invitation of the pastors. My husband never went to any city without the cooperation of its pastors.

Often our meetings drew church people together in a new way. Many churches which backed our meetings were fervently denominational. Some pastors thought that if one didn't believe exactly what they believed, one had no hope in God's eyes. Denominations kept themselves apart. People mixed and mingled within their own denominations, but that was all.

Our associate evangelist Bob DeWeese would say to the pastors, "You've invited Oral Roberts to come for a crusade, and these are his terms. You must invite all the churches in town which might be interested in helping to sponsor a crusade. You must get them all together and see how many are interested. If enough of them are interested and if you form a committee out of that group and all of you sign a letter of invitation, we will come. But Brother Roberts will not come for one church or one denomination. It has to be a city-wide effort and everybody who wants to be a part must have an opportunity.''

You know, the masses of people would have come whether their church pastors cooperated or not. It made no difference to them. They came because they were interested in hearing the gospel. But getting the pastors together was almost unprecedented. Many pastors have told us that our crusades marked the beginning of precious fellowship that they had never experienced before with pastors of other churches.

During the crusades, the pastors met for a meeting and prayer in the mornings. Bob DeWeese would speak to the people in the afternoon and tell them what to expect in the evening meeting and about the healing line. Many people had never before been to a healing service and didn't know what to expect. And Brother DeWeese told them how to release their faith and how and *why* to believe for healing when they came for prayer.

We had the main service in the evening.

The very first overseas crusade I attended

was in South Africa. I have never felt so inadequate in all my life. From 3,000 to 5,000 people stood when the invitation was given to accept the Lord and we had about one tenth as many counselors and prayer workers as we needed. Each of our team members tried to take at least ten persons to counsel and even that wasn't enough.

Charlotte DeWeese — wife of Bob — and I were praying with ten persons at a time as fast as we could and finally one night I just gave up and went to the prayer room by myself. In frustration I prayed, "Lord, somehow Your Spirit has got to get through to these people because there is no way that we can pray with each one of them."

We had enormous crowds, 30,000 and more daily. I couldn't conceive that people would come and sit in the rain with umbrellas all afternoon to save a seat for the evening meeting. South Africa had a law that Black people and white people had to stay separated, so the big arena was filled mainly with whites.

Oral had a strong desire to pray for the Black people, but there didn't seem to be anything we could do about the situation. Finally, some of our missionaries arranged for us to go out to a little town which had a large park. There the Black people came and stood all Saturday morning until my husband arrived. As soon as the morning service was over in the arena, we drove out to the park.

People were standing as far as we could see. Oral had to use three interpreters because several dialects were represented by the people. That didn't last long, though. He became frustrated waiting for three persons to translate each sentence before he could speak again, and finally he said, "I'm going to preach in English and somehow the Lord will help these people understand what I'm saying. I don't know how, but He will."

So he began preaching in English. I'm sure they did not understand his words, but somehow they understood the *meaning* of what he was telling them, and hundreds and hundreds of people raised their hands to accept Christ.

Oral couldn't pray for the people in a line so he prayed for them as mass. One schoolteacher ran up to the front wearing a neck brace shouting, "My neck has been healed!" She ripped off the neck brace and held it high! And, believe me, the people went absolutely wild. It was a rewarding experience to be in that meeting.

We stayed three weeks in South Africa and thousands of people were won to the Lord. Again, I felt my longing to be a missionary was fulfilled.

Often, as we traveled around the world, Oral preached to filled stadiums with 80,000 to 100,000 people in a single service! With crowds that large it seemed at times that all we did was preach the gospel, invite people to accept Christ, and have a prayer with them standing at the altar. We'd send them to a nearby field where counselors would work with them, but seldom did we receive follow-up reports. We were often left wondering how many of the people had actually found Christ.

I frequently felt restricted and inadequate because I couldn't speak the language of the people. If I gave a personal testimony I had to do it through an interpreter. I felt helpless. It troubled me that I couldn't walk up to people and ask them what their troubles were.

Many nights I'd ask Oral while we were driving back to the hotel, "Oh, Honey, do you think we've done any good at all? I feel so helpless. How do you ever know if the message is getting through?"

And Oral would always respond, "Evelyn, I can only give them the Word of God. And then I have to depend on the Spirit of God to send it to their hearts. That's the only way. God's Word will not return to Him void."

Two young missionary friends of ours, Sherry and Buddy, recently returned from Kenya. Sherry said to us, "I want to share some of the things that happened after your meeting in Nairobi several years ago."

"Oh, please tell me, please tell me."

"Did you know that about a thousand people among all those who were converted in your meetings united and built a new church? The first members were all people who met Jesus while you were in Kenya."

"No, I didn't know that. This is the first time I've heard that."

"We met people all over Nairobi and the surrounding area who accepted Jesus Christ in your crusade. They are beautiful Christians. Every time someone learns we are from the United States he says, 'Oh, do you know Brother Oral Roberts? It was through him that I found the Lord.' "

Sherry will never know how much her words meant to me!

I'm looking forward to meeting someday, face to face, those people who know the Lord through Oral's ministry. I don't think I'll *ever* stop rejoicing!

Mom of Robin Hood Farm

Six of the happiest years of our lives were spent on Robin Hood Farm, an acreage we purchased when our children were small. I can still see Richard and Roberta and our dog going toward the barn — Richard pulling Roberta in the red wagon, dumping her out, picking her up and wiping her tears. We had registered Angus cattle on Robin Hood Farm and it was a quiet place to rest between crusades and travels and to watch our children grow. I always looked forward to coming home.

I often tell students at Oral Roberts University that my husband has a talent to preach; Richard has a talent to sing; and everybody in our family can do something, except me. I'm left without any talents. But then it dawned on me: *When they all get hungry, they come to Mother.* And that made me feel good. Oral says, "Evelyn, I believe you would rather feed the children than do anything else I have ever seen you do." I figure that's the only talent I have, so why not use it as a way to show my love.

I enjoy being a woman — a wife and mother and grandmother. I believe the highest calling of a woman is motherhood. To have entrusted into her care the life of a precious child is to me one of earth's sweetest joys, greatest privileges, and heaviest responsibilities. When you consider that you are rearing a life for eternity, it is indeed a sobering thought.

Dr. Myron Sackett, an associate of ours for many years prior to his death, wrote a letter to me once when he was in Jerusalem. He said:

This morning as I was praying, you came to my mind and I prayed for you, and I feel impressed to write to you and tell you what a blessing you and your darling children have been and are to me. With the type of work Oral is doing, I'm sure it is a hardship on him to be away from his

130

family so much. And naturally this has shifted more responsibility on your shoulders in the raising of the family.

But what a reward will be waiting for you and Oral both! For as you have accepted this responsibility to do your part in raising and training your beautiful, Christian children, you have freed Oral to bring healing and deliverance to millions. I feel you and Oral will share and share alike in God's great rewards.

This letter is precious to me because it reminds me that being a good wife and mother *is something important.* I was fulfilled and I felt useful. I can't understand women who feel that being "just a housewife and mom" isn't enough. I suppose it depends on who you are and what you try to do, but being a "mom" was a full-time job for me and I loved my work. I love my home. I love to cook and do all the homey things a mother does. I love children.

I don't believe there are "bad" children. The Bible tells us that every good and perfect gift is from above, and since children come from God, they are good. They misbehave sometimes, but with proper training and a lot of love and understanding, I believe children can never get away from the things they are taught when they are small.

It was my job to help my children form good habits, and I worked hard to keep them on schedules as regular as our irregular life would allow. I stressed proper nutrition almost as fervently as I stressed spiritual values. The body is the temple of the spirit.

When the children were all home, I cooked a huge breakfast with hot biscuits and bacon and scrambled eggs, and oftentimes gravy to go with the biscuits. (You have to live in Oklahoma to understand that!) The boys, especially, would come to the table and say, "Mother, don't you have biscuits this morning? Oh, Mother. . . ." I had to have biscuits almost every morning.

I admit I catered to them a little too much. Rebecca didn't like eggs so I fixed her something else. But breakfast was a habit in our family. I felt a good breakfast was a big factor in physical health and we had very few doctor bills when the children were growing up.

Our mornings probably would have been a lot easier if I hadn't felt so strongly about breakfast. We almost had a "breakfast brigade."

The children went to school in a nearby town for a few years, but it was much easier to "single out" Oral Roberts's children in a small school and this was not what we wanted. One teacher gave Rebecca straight A's, and Rebecca was not a straight-A student. Now if Ronnie had received straight A's, I wouldn't have thought anything about it because he was a "brain." Rebecca was a *good* student, but not *that* good. When Rebecca showed me her report card, I said, "Rebecca, there's something wrong."

"I know it, Mother. Isn't that great! I don't have to study at all and I get straight A's."

"No, that's not right. You're not learning anything that way. I'm going to talk to the teacher." So I went to the school and the teacher said, "Well, she's just a good student."

I felt in my heart, though, that something was not fair. Oral and I talked it over and decided it was our obligation to give our children the best and *fairest* education we could. We decided to transfer them to a larger school in Tulsa. This meant a fifteen-mile drive into town each morning for them. Ronnie's classes started at 7:30 A.M. and he had to catch a bus at 6:30. By that time, he and I had shared a hot breakfast and had gone to the bus stop that was over a mile from our house.

After Ronnie was on the bus, I came back home and cooked breakfast for the other children and got them off to school. Many times I drove them into town myself. Our offices were in downtown Tulsa, too, so some days I made three trips to Tulsa, taking the children to school, going to the office, and taking one or more of the children to a school or church function in the evening. I felt like a chauffeur. (Don't many mothers?)

After the children were off to school, I'd prepare a third breakfast for Oral if he was home and have a cup of coffee with him. This was always a special time for us. And for me, it was a breather. I'd been up and busy for several hours.

When Oral was at home, he always seemed to be out in the yard playing with the children. He loves to ride horses. When the boys were small, he used to ride with one or both of the boys mounted behind him. When Richard was about three years old, Oral put the horse into a trot and little Richard's head kept bobbing back and forth, hitting his father on the back.

"Keep your head still, Richard."

"Aw-right."

But the little head kept right on bobbing and thumping Oral.

"Richard Lee, I said to keep your head still."

The horse kept a steady trot and Richard's little head kept a steady bump, bump. When Oral told him the third time to keep his head still, Richard replied, "Daddy, it won't 'tay 'till." And who could argue that point?

Mothers frequently ask me for advice about how to bring up their children. I didn't solve all the problems as a mother, but I think the best advice I can give is this: Get a good grip on the Lord. Know Him for yourself. Know how to talk to Him for yourself. Then saturate your children with the Word of God. They can't stray too far when the Word is rooted and grounded in them. If children are not taught at home and grounded in their faith, their innocent minds become fertile soil for someone to come along and plant in them one of the Satan-inspired ideologies that abound today.

The world will make a desperate bid for our children and their minds. We can't stop this. But while they are in our care and under our control, we can build up an arsenal of Scripture and faith in their minds against which the very gates of hell cannot prevail.

We usually had our family devotions at night, but there was no rigid pattern or set rule. Many times, a need in the family would create a special time for prayer and Bible discussion. Oral and I felt, too, that regimented devotions might become commonplace and we wanted prayer and Bible reading to be spontaneous. Occasionally I read them Scriptures or put a promise box on the table. Sometimes we prayed together and at times I went to each bedroom and prayed individually with each child.

I feel that a child should learn how to talk to Jesus as a friend and to depend on Him to get needs met. I wanted the children to become spiritually independent and learn how to go to the Scriptures themselves.

Many times, when the children have come to me with a problem, I've asked them, "Have you prayed about it? Have you asked the Lord what to do?"

I usually taught them Sunday school lessons on Saturday night so they would be sure to know them the next morning.

Rebecca used to say, "You have to be near death's door to miss Sunday school at our house."

I'm so grateful to Oral, too, for instilling the Scriptures in our children. From the time the children were able to talk, their father took them on his knee and told them Bible stories and had them learn and recite Scripture verses. I can almost hear Roberta's answer when we asked her, "Roberta, who is Jesus?"

"He's the Savior of the *Wold.*"

When each of the children reached his or her eighth birthday, Oral gave the child a Bible, inscribed it, and said, "I want you to read a chapter out of your own Bible every day of your life." I've often seen the children go to sleep with their Bibles cradled in their arms.

Of course, our children were brought up believing in the power of prayer. When Richard and Roberta were very small they would listen to our radio programs each Sunday. Oral would always say on the programs, "Now if you want to be prayed for, and there's no one in the room whom you can touch as your point of contact, put your hand on the radio."

Oral might be sitting there in the room with us when the program was aired, but Richard would say, "Come on, Roberta, put your hands on the radio now." And they would go to the radio and touch it together. Oral would just look at me and shake his head.

One Sunday morning while we were on

the way to Sunday school, Roberta asked, "Mother, what day is this?"

I said, "It's the first day of the new year. And, you know, Jesus may come before this year ends."

"Why is He coming?"

"To take us all to heaven with Him."

"Well, why does He want to take us to heaven with Him?"

"He wants to get us out of this wicked, mean world."

"Oh, it isn't a mean world."

Richard spoke up, "Oh, Roberta, you just haven't been downtown."

All our children went with us often to the crusades. We felt that this was a part of their education. They'd take their school homework with them and study during the day and we would all go to the meetings at night.

Getting a good education was as important in our home as breathing. Perhaps it was the "teacher" in me, but I wanted my children to like school and be excited about learning new things.

As each child got old enough to hold a book and look at pictures, I put books in their hands. I can remember Richard lying in his baby bed when he was just old enough to turn the pages of a book. He'd lie on his back and cross his legs and turn page after page until his eyes closed and he was asleep.

Ronnie and Roberta are our two college graduates. Ronnie was granted a Woodrow Wilson Fellowship for graduate work and Roberta was regularly on the honor roll in college.

It was a rule in our home: *No television until homework is done.* If there was any period between the time the children finished their homework and bedtime, they might get to see one program. They all had fixed bedtimes.

On weekends we rented a film that was acceptable and invited all the neighbors in. We all enjoyed westerns. We'd pop corn and have a prayer time afterwards — and have just a wonderful time each week.

For a long time we rented a serial about Wild Bill Hickok and each week we showed a different chapter. The children could hardly wait to see what would happen to Wild Bill next!

Having movies in our home was our way of dealing with a fairly sensitive problem that arose when our children's friends began inviting our children to attend movies.

Oral said, "Evelyn, I think you should screen the movies they want to see and if you think they are okay, let them go with their friends." He also called in Ronnie and Rebecca, who were the first ones who wanted to go, and said, "Your mother and I feel that if you want to see a movie, you should read all the reviews very carefully to make sure you know what the movie is about. If you still feel that as a Christian you want to see it, then you may go. You must take the responsibility and make your own decisions."

The children were very careful about what they chose, and they read the newspaper reviews regularly. Sometimes we stopped them from going to see something, but usually we allowed them to exercise their own judgment.

The Fourth of July was a special occasion in our family. Since Robin Hood Farm was outside of the city limits, we could have aerial fireworks. They were always so beautiful. And so were the freezers filled with homemade ice cream!

One summer Ronnie went to camp at my urging because I wanted him to learn to live with other children his own age and become more independent. I primed him with stories about swimming, horseback riding, hikes, and picnics until he gave in and agreed to go. Rebecca and I packed his clothes, sheets, pillow, blankets, and swimsuit, and drove him over to Arkansas. We stayed just long enough for him to meet his roommate and get acquainted with two or three other boys. I unpacked his clothes, made his bed, and gave him some spending money, and left feeling that this would be *one* camp he would enjoy. I felt he'd have the opportunity to meet people from other parts of the country and that he'd learn from them.

I hadn't reckoned with the fact that July Fourth was coming up.

Ronnie wrote from summer camp:

Dear Mother:
I want to please come home when

142

this week is over. I am not homesick, but I don't like this place very much. Please come and get me Saturday, the fourth. *Please! Please! Please! Please!*

Ronnie Roberts

P.S. I want to come home Saturday!! *Please! Please!*

Jack, a big, tough Texan who managed the farm and lived nearby, had brought me the mail. After I read Ronnie's letter, I handed it to him. Big tears began to roll down his cheeks and he said, "I'm going after that boy. You just call him and tell him to pack his clothes. If he wants to be home on July Fourth, I'll see that he gets here." And he drove 200 miles that day to bring Ronnie home for the fireworks and ice cream.

Richard was the most daring child we had. He wasn't afraid of anything. The lack of fear was partly Oral's fault.

I was preparing dinner one summer evening while all the family were swimming when Oral stuck his head in the door and said, "Evelyn, come here, I want you to see something." Richard was about five and there he was standing on the diving board. I almost had a heart attack. Oral said, "Jump, Richard." And while I gasped, Richard jumped in and learned to swim.

There is a closeness among our children that's difficult to explain. One semester during high school, Rebecca went away to Bible school. She wrote, "I'm not homesick, but I'm lonesome to see Bertie [Roberta], Richie, and everybody. Lots of love."

Every time one of the children was away, he or she always wrote about missing the others.

That isn't to say they always got along when they were together! We had our fair share of squabbles.

When Roberta was little, she clashed with everybody. She's always been very sensitive. She clashed with Ronnie and Richard as much as she clashed with anybody else because she was fat when she was little and they called her Fatso. She hated every minute of it. At the table, they'd pass something to her and say, "Here, give it to Fatso." She was so sensitive she'd get up from the table and run to her bedroom and close the door and never eat one bite.

Richard teased her constantly. He was only two years older and loved her dearly. No one else could say anything about her or he'd put on his fighting clothes, but he loved to pester her himself. If he couldn't get a rise out of her any other way, he would just put his foot out and trip her.

She couldn't stand him. She'd say, "Mother, I hate him. Mother, one of these days I'm going to hurt Rich and I'm going to hurt him bad. Mother, I hate him!" (Of course this feeling changed and Roberta adores him now.)

The children were sincerely concerned about the success of one another. In one letter, Ronnie said, "Richard, I do hope your grades are at least average. It can put a damper on life to be weighed down by a miserable high school transcript. Worrying about grades is drudgery, I know, but you owe yourself a chance to use your mind. I'm convinced that you do have a superior mind." Ronnie never doubted for a minute that Richard could make good grades.

Ronnie was a straight-A student and I

had no problem getting him to do his homework. But then Richard came along and he hated to study. He wanted to ride bicycles, play with the dog, play ball (he knew the statistics of every major league ball player), or play golf. He could remember every golf stroke for an entire eighteen holes, but he couldn't remember his arithmetic. I'd get notes from his teacher about his "attention span."

We worried about Richard and one time I said, "Richard, why can't you be like your brother?" That was a terrible thing to say and I've had to repent for it many times. If only we had realized that everyone has his own talent. Arithmetic wasn't Richard's talent, but that didn't mean he couldn't do other things.

Ronnie posted a note on his door one day when he was about eleven or twelve. It said, "Private." He wanted to work on his school lessons and Richard was told to stay out of sight so Ronnie could concentrate. Richard came to me and said, *"I* want a sign. Ronnie is consecratin' and I want to consecrate, too!"

Oral and I, too, sometimes disagree. We

have our own opinions and we let them be known.

I suppose there is a dream car in the mind of every man. Oral's dream car was a convertible. One day he drove up in a brand-new convertible and enthusiastically ran in to say, "Evelyn, come see what I bought."

When I saw it, I was shocked.

"Oral, have you bought this without talking it over with me?"

"Yes, I've always wanted a convertible. The guy gave me a good deal and I took it."

"Is this to be the family car?"

"Yes."

"Well, you can take it right back, because *my* children will not ride in a convertible to be killed."

I shall never forget how crestfallen he looked. He really wanted that car.

The Lord knew I was sincere and Oral knew it, too, so he returned the car. That's one of the few times I've ever gone that far with a disagreement.

In spite of Oral's traveling, he and I worked constantly to build a feeling of security and stability in our home. I think children suffer when they lose their feelings of security. Some parents turn their children loose and let them do whatever they want to do. They go where they want to go. There's no discipline. I don't believe you can have security without discipline. And so many of the homes in our country are broken already by divorce. Many children are without a strong father figure. The mothers are raising the children without a father, and boys especially need a feeling of discipline that comes from a father.

I know our children felt Oral and I were hard on them, but they never doubted our stand on what we felt was right. When we had family discussions, all of this came out.

Usually I disciplined the children because I had to. But there were times when I waited for Oral to come home. He often accused me of meeting him at the door with, ''Here's a switch. Whip these children.''

He said, ''My children hate to see me come in the door because they know you are going to say, 'Switch these children.

They've been acting bad since you've been gone.' "

I'm sure it may have seemed that way at times, but there were some things for which I felt *he* should discipline them. I wanted the children to know that their father didn't approve of some of the things they were doing. And I wanted them to know that he was as much of a disciplinarian as I was.

In many ways, we were as "ordinary" as a family can be. We ate together, played together, prayed together. We had our individual strengths, but we worked at being a united family. And being the mother in a normal family routine on a farm in Oklahoma suited me just fine.

Helpmate for
a Growing Ministry

My husband calls me his inspiration, and I hope I am. That's all I've ever wanted to be as Mrs. Oral Roberts.

I like the word "companion" and the Bible word "helpmate" (Genesis 2:18). I want to do everything I can to encourage and help Oral. I'm a wife, a mother, a grandmother, and have done all the things those titles imply — from paying bills to changing diapers. But my role as a helpmate has included a variety of *other* positions. Most of them I've really enjoyed. Some of them have involved doing some things I never thought I could do.

The year Oral began his crusade ministry (1947) almost became the last. We were conducting a crusade in the Memorial Auditorium in Chanute, Kansas. The crowds were coming, people were being helped, but the expenses were not being met. One night Oral closed his Bible, walked off the platform and said, "Lord, I have made a mistake; I'm going home."

When his brother, Vaden, came and told me, I went as fast as I could to where Oral was standing behind the curtain on the platform.

"Oral, I know it is hard but you can't quit now!"

"Evelyn, you know my vow. I promised I would never touch the gold nor the glory. We do not have money enough to meet our budget. If God had really called me, He would meet our needs. The needs are not met and I am going home."

But I knew something, too. God had called Oral to this ministry. There was no doubt in my mind. Since Oral felt he could not personally ask the people again for the needs of the meeting, I felt it was up to me to do what I could to help.

Without saying a word to him, I stepped out onto the platform. I frankly told the people what the situation was. Then I picked up a man's hat and took an offering. God spoke to their hearts and there was a spontaneous response that warmed our hearts as well as paid the bill. Never had I done such a thing before — nor have I since. That wasn't at all "my style" — but it was something I felt compelled to do in that moment. Oral and I both learned then and there that if people really know there is a need they are quick to want to be a part of God's work.

In addition to that one job as a hat passer, I've often had the occupations of letter writer, chauffeur, stamp licker, and mail sorter.

Some of the most thrilling days I have known were those days of faith and hard work in the expanding crusade ministry. As our radio ministry began, letters started coming to our house at the rate of forty to sixty a day. Our home became an office and a prayer chapel. We ate very few meals without calls from desperate people who pleaded for Oral's prayers.

Three young women who wanted to help in the Lord's work volunteered to come to our home in the evenings to type the answers to the letters. One of these young women, Ruth Rooks, became executive secretary to Oral and has been with us over twenty-five years. There is no way to describe with words what Ruth has meant to both of us over the years. She was "sent by God," I feel sure.

Through the mail, testimonies began to come from people whose lives were changed. A healing had taken place or some special miracle had happened in their lives. It blessed us so much to read their letters that we felt others would be blessed too. So, for twenty-five years, I have read many of these testimonies on our radio broadcasts.

When Oral was at home, my helping often meant protecting him as much as possible from public demands. I was his guardian of privacy. (That was one helping job I didn't mind.)

But while traveling in the crusades, he led a lonely life unless I could manage to be with him at least part of the time.

On occasion, I have had the privilege of witnessing both about Christ and my husband. I shall never forget one summer when the children and I had leased a cottage on the beach in California. One afternoon

Richard walked into the house and said, "Mother, there is a man at the door to see you."

At the door I saw a big, portly gentleman with a cigar in his pocket. He spoke to me in broken English. "Lady, have you heard of a man in this area by the name of Oral Roberts?"

"Yes," I said, "I've heard of him."

"Well, what about him — is he a good neighbor?"

This nearly floored me for suddenly I realized the man did not know who I was. After a little hesitation, I answered, "Yes, I think he is a good neighbor. Why do you ask?"

"My wife and I have been watching him on television. I just happened to mention to one of my neighbors that I had been watching him, and he said to me, 'Oh, don't watch him. That man is a drunkard.'"

"What?"

"Yes, he's a drunkard. My friend told me he knows it for a fact."

"And how does he know this?"

"Because he saw him at the airport — so drunk he could hardly walk."

I said, "You had better be able to prove a thing like that before you go spreading it around."

"Well," the man continued, "I said to my wife, 'If I'm ever close to where he is, I will inquire about Oral Roberts. I don't believe those wild tales.' So I heard he had a cottage here for the summer and I have inquired and the people I ask say Oral Roberts is a good man, and now you say he is a good neighbor."

At that point, I figured I surely had heard everything. My husband being accused of being drunk!

I looked at this gentleman, who was honestly seeking for something to strengthen his faith in the man he had watched on television preaching about God's healing power. I said to him, "Sir, I know Mr. Roberts quite well and I can tell you for a fact he lives what he preaches. I've known him twenty years and I have never seen him touch a drop of liquor and he has never told me a lie."

"Are you Mrs. Roberts?" he gulped.

"Yes, sir, I am."

"And you let me run on about your

husband and didn't try to stop me? Mrs. Roberts, please come to the car and meet my wife."

After I met his wife and we talked a while about the goodness of God and of my husband's sincerity, my new-found friend asked me, "Will you please ask Brother Roberts to pray for me? I have gall-bladder trouble and the doctors say they will have to operate."

People often ask me questions when I'm traveling to meet my husband. I am usually carrying my Bible with me, and people who sit next to me invariably ask, "Are you a minister?"

"No."

"Missionary?"

"No."

"Then why do you have the Bible?"

"Well, I'm a Christian and I like to use my flying time to catch up on Bible reading. I have many times read whole books of the Bible while in flight."

This kind of conversation often gives me an opportunity to talk about the Lord.

On one flight to North Carolina, I was trying to read but found it difficult because a man about my age kept asking me questions. He was getting a little too chummy and I was annoyed, so I finally said, "Sir, have you ever watched a minister on television by the name of Oral Roberts?"

He looked at me quickly and said, "Oh, yes, many times."

"He is my husband," I announced, "and I am on my way to meet him where he is holding a crusade."

The man turned in his seat, lifted himself halfway up and put out his hand. "Well, Mrs. Roberts, it is indeed an honor to sit by you. My wife will never believe I sat by you — she'll think I'm lying."

I gave him a card with my name and a verse of Scripture on it to give to his wife. From that moment on he was a perfect gentleman and we had a good conversation about the Lord.

And, in my position as a helpmate, I've even been a golf caddy.

During one of the crusades, the weather turned bad and Oral had to stay inside much of the time, so he called and asked me to come and bring his nine-iron golf club with me. I suppose he was going to practice swinging it or something. Anyway, neither the children nor I could decide which was the nine and which was the six. The surest way of getting him the one he wanted, I concluded, was to take both of them with me.

Well, this created quite a sensation on the plane. But I've learned after all these years that Oral Roberts creates a scene even when he isn't present. Curiosity got the best of one of my fellow passengers. He got up from his seat, came to me, and said, "Excuse me, lady, but my wife and I have been having quite a discussion about you. We have been trying to decide if you are on your way to a golf tournament and if so, how do you play with just two clubs?"

Someone recently said Oral Roberts has held jobs of over fifty titles in his life — from paper boy to university president — and I think I've held just about as many by being his helpmate for a growing ministry. For love of God — and Oral Roberts.

No Ordinary Marriage

"Evelyn, there's something wrong in our marriage."

I couldn't believe my ears. There sat my Christian husband — loving father of my children — telling me we had a problem in our marriage. The tone of his voice and the troubled look on his face told me he was serious.

Something inside me said, "What do *you* know about marriage? You're away most of the time! We're apart as much as, or more than, we're together. It certainly isn't *my* idea to have a commuting marriage."

I was defensive, but I was also hurt. Yet it was funny. I *loved* Oral and the times we could be together seemed happy and wonderful to me. I had accepted the fact that ours was to be a lifetime of giving and sharing. I had learned to deal with times when I wanted him to myself, but couldn't have him. I thought we had adjusted.

I felt we had reached a balance. . . .

During the first few years of our ministry, Oral was gone sometimes three weeks out of four. At first I divided my time between him and the children — having someone come in to stay with them while I attended part of the crusade.

On one long overseas trip, Oral asked me to join him for the last week or so. Richard did not want me to go. When we returned, we discovered that Richard had taken his hatchet and chopped off the bedpost. When we asked him why, he said, "Well, Mother, I told you not to go overseas. And you went anyway, so I just thought, *'Okay, if Mother goes overseas, I'll just chop up my bed!'*" And he did.

After that, my time became more and more one-sided. I felt the children needed at least one parent around most of the time in case of emergencies.

I felt we had learned to deal with fear. . . .

One time, when Oral was in a crusade in Virginia, I had quite a scare. The children and I were alone in the house. About three o'clock in the morning I awakened suddenly. Someone was trying to break into the house. I became paralyzed with fear.

My first thought was to be quiet so I wouldn't awaken the children and frighten them. I thought of calling the police, but I was too scared to find the number. I kept thinking, "Oh, if Oral were only here!"

I sat up on the side of the bed and started praying. I asked the Lord to let Oral know that we were in trouble because I knew if he prayed, everything would be all right. Within a few minutes I was as calm as could be. A sweet peace engulfed me.

The noise had stopped and I knew whoever was trying to break in was gone. I went back to sleep.

In about a week, Oral came home and I told him about someone's trying to break in. He began to smile.

"What's so funny?" I asked, a little perturbed because he was taking it lightly.

"Evelyn," he answered, "was this about three o'clock on Tuesday morning?"

"Well, yes. But how did you know? I haven't told you that part yet."

Then he told me that at that exact hour he was awakened and was sure that someone had called him and told him to get up. He turned on the light and searched the room. Finding no one, he returned to his bed and sat down. A clear picture came to him of the children and me in danger. For a moment all he could do was picture us in danger so far away. Then he dropped down on his knees and prayed to the Lord. "I am fourteen hundred miles away from my family. I can't get there to help them. Please send an angel to protect them."

Then Oral felt peaceful and he knew that God had answered his prayer and all was well. Talk about today's jet-set travel! God's angels are much faster. I'm sure that an angel was at our home before Oral had finished his prayer — clasping my hand in Tulsa and Oral's hand in Virginia, closing the distance and bringing us together to restore peace.

After he told me this, he said, "Honey, don't ever be afraid again. God is awake all night long watching over you."

"You should say that in every sermon you preach." I exclaimed. "People need to hear it over and over."

More than fear, I knew how hard we both had worked at keeping from feeling lonely. . . .

The longest weeks of my life have been those when Oral is not with me. I want him near to me, as any other wife wants her husband. Still, I know it has been much harder for Oral to be away from home than for me to have him away. I at least had the children. He had no one. He stayed in a lonely hotel room, rarely leaving except to get some exercise, eat his meals, and go to the tent at night.

People often ask me how a *minister* could get homesick overseas when the Lord was blessing him. I think they forget that a minister is human. I don't think we like our ministers to be human.

In one letter, Oral wrote, "Although homesick, I'm just fine. The people received me as if I were an angel. Their faces mirrored every feeling and they hung on evry word I said. The anointing was so strong that my native interpreter began weeping and had to be replaced. They knew that I loved them."

When Oral was in the pulpit ministering, the homesickness left him. But when he'd leave the pulpit and the anointing would subside, he'd go back to his room where he was very much a human being. And human beings, perhaps *especially* ministers, get lonely.

The separation from the children was just as hard. I remember in one letter he said, "I envy you, Evelyn, for you get to see the children. Kiss them double for me. There is only one power that keeps me away from them: this burning urge in my soul that God put there. Seems sometimes it will consume me; I feel it so deeply. . . ."

It wasn't easy for Rebecca and Ronnie to get used to having their daddy away either. Often one of them would say, "Mother, why does Daddy have to be gone all of the time?"

"Well, Honey," I would answer, "he is out trying to win souls to Jesus. He'll be home soon."

But the "soon" I mentioned never seemed soon enough for them, or for me. One day Ronnie asked me, "Mother, when is 'soon'?"

While I was at home and Oral was away at a crusade, I would often look at the clock to know exactly what he was doing. I knew his schedule so well. He lived by the clock and I could follow his movements all day.

I knew what time he ate breakfast. In the morning, he usually had to write an article for the magazine, answer special mail, work on a new book, or be interviewed by the press. Usually he would go out for some exercise, eat a bowl of soup at noon, then return to his room for an afternoon of meditation, study, and prayer. He took no calls and had no contact with anyone except the Lord from two thirty to five thirty. Then he went out for dinner and returned to the room until it was time to preach.

Oral liked to eat as quickly as possible so his line of thought wouldn't be broken. His mind would be on his message and he would talk very little. He disliked waitresses who stalled; he wanted his meals *immediately* so he could get back to his room.

When Richard was about three years old, I was packing to go to one of the crusades and I asked him if he would like to go with me. "No," he said, "Daddy just 'tuddies [studies] and prays all the time."

I knew how excited we all got about Daddy's coming home. . . .

When he'd leave, our house wouldn't be normal for two weeks. The came the time for him to come home again and everybody came alive. We'd cook and clean house and get so excited we could hardly wait. The children would go with me to the airport and they'd jump up and down as soon as they'd see the plane start to land. It was all I could do to hold them until the door was opened and their daddy would start down the steps. "Visitors Stay Behind Fence" signs were always ignored.

I knew how we had adjusted even the births *of our children around Oral's ministry schedule. . . .*

Richard was expected about November 10, 1948. Oral was holding a crusade in Dallas and he called me long distance to say, "Evelyn, this meeting is wonderful. I don't see how I can close it in time to be home on Wednesday when our baby is expected." He said, "Honey, can you put off having the baby for a day or two? I need to continue the meeting until Wednesday night. I could be home on Thursday."

No one but Oral Roberts would ask his wife to do what Oral asked me.

I didn't doubt that the Lord could answer this request. I had simply never asked Him to do anything like this and I said to Oral, "Well, the Lord will have to help me."

He said, "Let's agree in prayer that the baby will not arrive until Thursday."

"No, you will be too tired to stay at the hospital on Thursday after just getting home," I said. "Since we are going to ask the Lord to change the time, let's set the time for Friday before midnight."

Sure enough, on Friday at 6 P.M. Oral and I went to Hillcrest Hospital. The doctor told us it would take all night. Oral and I knew differently. The baby would arrive before midnight. After all, we had asked God about it and we had asked it because Oral was busy helping people and this would fit his schedule better.

The men in the waiting room laughed when Oral said it would happen before midnight. They said, "Get comfortable, mister. Some of us have been here two nights and a day."

At exactly 11:20 P.M., forty minutes before midnight, the nurse went out and told Oral that he had a son. One of the men in the waiting room said, "Can you beat that?"

Things were just as extraordinary when our fourth child, Roberta Jean, was born. As usual, Oral went to the hospital with me, taking along with him his writing material. He was working to finish two new books: *The Fourth Man* and *Oral Roberts's Life Story*. In the fathers' waiting room, Oral began to write. One of the fathers who was also keeping vigil asked, "What are you writing?"

"A book," Oral answered and went right on writing.

"What kind of a book?"

"Oh, just a book."

"Does it have anything to do with religion?"

"Yes."

"What is your name?"

"Roberts."

"Could it be Oral Roberts?"

"Yes, I am Oral Roberts."

About this time the man's wife came in the room. She had been there twenty-four hours already. Her baby was due, but she was having a very long labor.

The man whispered to his wife, she whispered back to him, started out the door, but changed her mind and came back. She walked straight to Oral and said, "Are you him?"

"Am I who?"

"Oral Roberts — are you Oral Roberts, *in person?*"

It was amusing the way it happened, but at a glance Oral knew she was not trying to be humorous. She was very serious.

Oral said, "Do you know me?"

"Yes, my mother has been to your meetings. She has told me about your great faith. Brother Roberts, can you help me? I have been here so long and they say I may have to wait another twenty-four hours."

Oral called her husband and asked them to join hands. They began to pray. He discerned her terrible fear, so he started talking to her in his calm but vibrant voice — in a tone he used in speaking to his own children.

"Little lady," he was saying, "having a baby is the most natural thing in the world for a woman. God made you like that. You can have your baby by noon if you will ask and believe God."

"I have been so scared," she confided. "Do you really believe that?"

"Yes," Oral said with assurance, "I know it. Now go, and the Lord will be with you."

Her baby, a boy, was born five minutes before noon — twenty minutes before our Roberta Jean made her arrival. As they rolled her out of the labor room, they rolled me in and she looked across at me and said, "I beat you — I had mine before noon, just as your husband said." And a big smile flashed across her face.

And I knew how hard we worked to make everything right when Oral was home. . . .

Rebecca is a lot like Oral when it comes to food likes and dislikes. Whatever he likes to eat, she likes to eat. When it was time for Oral to come home from a crusade, I'd ask Rebecca, "Now, Rebecca, if you had been eating in a restaurant for a long time, what would you want for dinner when you came home?" She'd tell me and I'd fix the nicest dinner I could.

Oral was extremely tired when he came home and dinner conversations sometimes went like this:

Oral: "My, this tastes awful. What did you put in this?"

Evelyn: "Well, Honey, I don't know. Doesn't it taste good? It's your favorite dish."

Oral: "No, it isn't my favorite dish. Would you mind telling me why you never have me in mind when you prepare a meal?"

Rebecca looked at me as if to say, "Mother, how can you stand it? How can you put up with this?"

Well, I let it go in one ear and out the other. I knew that when Oral came home he was tired; he was irritable. I knew, too, when he was relaxed and rested, food would be food again, so I didn't let this conversation disturb me.

However, on one such evening, Oral

said to me, "Put the children to bed. I have to talk to you."

After the children were in bed, I joined him in the den and he closed the door. "Now, Evelyn, I want to tell you something. *There is something wrong in our marriage.*"

All of those *unusual* things in our marriage went through my mind in an instant, but I wasn't sure what was going on in *his* mind. I said, "There is? *What?*"

"Well, when I come home, you don't pay enough attention to me. You are with the children all the time and don't care what I want or what I do. You don't even know I'm in the house."

"Why, Honey, I plan and plan — the longest time — about things to do with you when you come home."

"No, you don't."

"Oral, I tell you, it's *you* who are the problem. You don't know what a normal marriage is like."

"I don't want a normal marriage. If it can't be better than normal, I don't want it. It has got to be *above* normal. I want us always to be sweethearts." And then he said, "Evelyn, there is no other woman

172

in this world that I want but you. And I want you to pay some attention to me."

I could have laughed, he was so serious, but I didn't dare. I had to sit on his lap and promise him that I would go with him wherever he went and do everything with him when he was home. This was what he wanted and this was what made him happy. And this was what I did.

Everywhere he went during that stay at home, I went too. When he got in the car to go to town, I went with him. When he went down to the barn to see the cows, I went with him. Wherever he went I was by his side. And he was happy.

There have also been times when he came home so exhausted, he wanted to be left completely alone — no talking, no companionship, nothing — until he was rested. I had to learn to understand his moods and still have to.

These are the things that have kept our marriage alive. We've both worked at it and tried not to take each other for granted.

He wanted a marriage that was better than normal — a marriage for sweethearts.

Oral and I often have "prayer meetings"

in which just he and I and the Lord meet and harmonize our thinking and planning. These are precious moments when two persons whose lives have become one can also blend into a oneness with the heavenly Father's will. These moments keep our marriage happy and help us harmonize the job of living both a public and private life consistently and abundantly.

We have acquired a habit of raiding the refrigerator together before bedtime. These late-night snacks are usually occasions for heart-to-heart talks about our future, and just about being in love. Over a glass of milk and Oral's nightly bowl of corn flakes we grow closer.

We try to keep the communication lines open. We talk about what we're doing and what we think and how we feel. Just recently I hurt Oral's feelings deeply and I couldn't get through to him by simply telling him I was sorry. I had to write a note and leave it where he would see it. Oral understands things better when they are written down. Here is what I wrote:

Oral darling: I want to say to you on

paper what I tried to say to you earlier when you were in no condition to listen with your heart. I am sorry I said I wanted to be alone awhile. I certainly did not mean that I don't enjoy being with you, because I do immensely. Some day I'll learn to keep my big, fat mouth shut. Years ago when you traveled in the crusades, I looked forward so much to your coming home. And sometimes it seemed all you wanted the first few days was to be alone to rest and relax.

Now in the last three or four years things seem to have reversed. You now want to be with me all the time. And now there are times when *I* want to be alone. I'm not as flexible as I used to be and I can't go back twenty years. I've never wanted to be with any other man, and never expect to. However, I still have to face the fact that my habits have changed. Now I need time alone to rest.

When I tell you, you're crushed. It doesn't mean that I love you any less. My life is tied to you much more than

I'm ever able to say in words. Others know, especially our children.

I have hurt all day because I hurt you. And I say sincerely, it was the last thing in my mind to hurt you. Unfortunately, I'm human and I offend when I don't intend to. I do love you.

I knew somebody had to take the first step in keeping the communication open and this time it was my turn.

I sometimes wonder just how many marriages could be salvaged or made happier if the partners would refuse to settle for an "ordinary marriage." Maybe the "something that is wrong" is simply something that isn't "right enough." Maybe some husbands and wives need to recapture a sweetheart feeling that comes through giving and sharing and praying together.

I agree with Oral. I don't ever want a *normal* marriage again!

Coping with Controversy

One thing I've learned about Oral Roberts's impact on people — they are either for him 100 percent or against him 100 percent. I don't know *why* — only that this is the way it's always been. And unfortunately, some of the press has been against us more often than it has been for us.

We've had to learn to deal with controversy and what we considered unfair accusations since the day we began a ministry that emphasized healing. At the time we started the crusades, there was very little said in churches of all denominations about healing. Because we emphasized healing, we were opposed immediately, not only in the press and by those who did not understand God's miracle-working power — which can be expected — but also by our own church people. Our church bishop was dead set against our healing ministry from the beginning. When Oral asked to be relieved of his full-time pastorate, the advice from his supervisor was, "You'd better stay with a good thing, and avoid that *wild* stuff." Oral didn't get any encouragement from anybody in the world except his mother and his father and me. Without the Scriptures and the confirmation that the Lord gave him, I don't think he could have withstood the harsh criticism.

Controversy not only touched Oral, it affected our children's lives, too.

I often think of something my granddaughter Brenda said. She dropped a toy on her foot and it hurt. She looked up through her tears and said, "Munna, I wish we couldn't feel." Many times I've felt that way. When people have said bad things about Oral, it has hurt me. It still does. I've never gotten over that. It hurts me because I know that his *motives* are good. If other people knew his motives, they would not question or speak ill of him. But unless you live with a person you can't know his motives. You can read headlines about him and see him and hear rumors about him, but unless you know someone's *motive* you don't really know him at all.

I would say to the children when controversy arose, "We know that Daddy is honest. We know that he's trying to do what God has asked him to do, whether anybody believes him or not. And *you* have to do what God tells you to do. You have to live honestly before God."

And the children would often say back to me, "Now, don't take me wrong, Mother. I'm not ashamed of Daddy or what he's doing. I'm just getting tired of people asking me questions all the time."

Our children always wanted to be like everybody else. They never wanted to be on display. People would say to me, "Oh, aren't your children proud of their dad, and don't they want to be on stage and shine with him?" And I would say, "Oh, yes, they're proud of their dad, but no, they don't want to be up there at all!"

When guests would come to our home, Rebecca would always go to her bedroom and close the door. She'd say, "Mother, if you need me I'll be in my bedroom, but unless you need me, please don't call me." She didn't want to see people. She didn't want to be looked at and fawned over and judged as Oral Roberts's daughter. She wanted to be Rebecca — her own person.

Richard and Roberta have never had to bear what Rebecca and Ronnie had to bear, but even they have had their "controversial moments" about their father.

Richard told me once that while he was talking to a girl at school, she made an offhand remark about his dad that he didn't appreciate. He came home fuming and said, "Mother, before I knew it had my fist drawn. When I realized she was a girl and I couldn't hit her, I could hardly stand it. One more word and I might have knocked her for a loop." You see, where Ronnie might give you a tongue-lashing, Richard would literally knock you down. He has that old Roberts temper.

Roberta told me once that a girl stopped her in the hall one day at school and asked, "Oh, Roberta, by the way, I meant to ask you, can your dad really heal people?"

Roberta said, "No, can yours?" and walked on.

The children got questions like this all the time, and they grew tired of them. Criticism and controversy affected each of us in different ways.

I think the greatest hurt for me, though, was the way the press treated us when we were in Australia.

We had been invited to Australia by a group of ministers representing the full-gospel churches, who had received permission from the Australian government.

The city governments of both Sydney and Melbourne granted us free use of their beautiful city parks for the big eight-pole tent. The Australian people appeared hungry for God. It seemed a natural setting for a great crusade. We planned to spend the entire summer in Australia holding crusades and sent the tents and all our equipment ahead by ship.

Then some of the daily newspapers decided against us. Advance press stories greeted us as we opened the first crusade in Sydney. One reporter, who was reproved by a minister for his false reporting, said,

"We are not writing what we want to write, but what we are *told* to write."

In spite of that kind of press coverage, people came to the meetings eager, open, and ready for the gospel. They represented many different denominations. During the nine days of the first crusade, approximately 75,000 persons attended. The police cooperated splendidly and instructed our workers in the handling of the large crowds. Order was maintained and, with little exception, the people were reverent. Some 3,000 came forward in nine nights to give their hearts to God and many testified to miraculous healings.

The Melbourne meetings opened on an even larger scale than those in Sydney. With more than 10,000 present, it looked as though it might be the greatest opening night of all our crusades. Four hundred persons came forward at the altar call. A nurse who had come hundreds of miles for prayer for her deformed feet was marvelously healed.

The next morning the newspapers launched an all-out attack. Every conceivable ruse was used to mislead the people and keep them away from the meeting.

Heckling started during the service that night. People yelled out to interrupt during the preaching and prayer for the sick.

By Wednesday night it was obvious that the opposition was organized. Hecklers came to the front with the converts and screamed their defiance. Well-known Communist agitators were recognized moving about, stirring up the mob.

We began to realize the mob was not only against Oral, but against the Word of God. The hecklers hissed at the Scripture reading and defied persons to receive Christ as their personal Savior. They were anti-God and antireligion.

When the Wednesday night service was dismissed, the mob rushed to the back of the tent to get at Oral, but he had been rushed off the grounds with a police escort. They shook the car I was in, trying to upset it because they thought Oral was with me. When they discovered he wasn't, they quit.

I told Oral, "I don't want you to stay. They are going to do something terrible and someone is going to get hurt. I wish you would close the meeting and leave."

He replied, "Honey, as long as the people are finding God and are being healed, I can't leave."

People called me in the night and said, "You'd better get your husband out of town because we're going to kill him."

I went to bed very troubled. I had already packed everything earlier in the day because I felt I had been gone from the children far too long. And now I was leaving in the middle of a crisis. I told Oral, "I don't fear for your life because I believe the Lord will take care of you. I think you should take precautions and protect yourself as much as you can, but I believe the Lord will protect you."

But the next morning when the men came to take me to the airport, they brought a morning paper. The front page told how people had tried to burn our trucks in the middle of the night, and how they vowed they would now *set fire to the tent*. I said, "This is not right. If Australians do not want us here, then we should not endanger our equipment. There are thousands of people in the United States who want crusades and I don't feel our equipment should be destroyed here by people who don't care. The Lord said to wipe the dust off your feet if your message is not accepted in a place [Luke 10:8-12]. We don't have to stay here. We can go home. I don't think the meeting should go on."

When I reached the airport, I called Bob DeWeese, who was in charge of the meetings, and said, "Bob, the headline in the morning newspaper says 'Roberts's Tent To Be Burned Tonight.' I don't think the meeting should go on, Bob. I really don't. It isn't right for things like this to happen." (I didn't know at the time, but he and our staff had met and decided the same thing.)

And he said, "Well, what do you think we should do?"

I said, "I think you should get the pastors together and explain to them why we are leaving. I think they will understand because they already know what has happened. And then I think you should load the tent, truck all the equipment to Sydney, and load it on the ship. By this afternoon, everything should be off those grounds. I don't think people should have a chance to burn the tent."

Bob said, "I feel the same way. I've received a call from the insurance company and they advised us to leave, too. But what do you think Oral will say?"

I said, "I don't care what he says or thinks. At this point, we have to save our equipment and ourselves. There are other places that want meetings. You get the tent down and I'll answer to Oral."

I knew Oral could see only the lost and suffering and not those who were out to destroy him. Bob DeWeese and a crew of men took down the tent, loaded the truck, and drove to Sydney. I flew on to Sydney and Oral joined me there. When the people came for the afternoon meeting at Melbourne, the lot was empty. I was told later that some of the people wept together to think that their country would not let a servant of God hold meetings.

I want to add that only a *few* Australians were involved in this turmoil. Many thousands really wanted the crusades and for those people we are very grateful.

When we got off the plane in San

Francisco, the angry press stories had already reached America. We couldn't seem to leave that ugly experience behind us. The press in Australia had sensationalized our meetings, calling them a circus and Oral a clown. These stories were reprinted in American newspapers and it was embarrassing. I wrote in my diary, "What do you do when you've given your life to God's work, left your children, and done everything you know to do for the Lord, and then are misrepresented?"

I have to be honest and say that I really felt the Lord had let us down — especially when the stories appeared in the United States newspapers. I was humiliated. (I have since learned to be more like St. Paul, who said he counted it a joy to be deemed worthy to be persecuted for the Christian faith he held dear.)

But when something like Australia — or anything bad — happens, I think it's our nature as men and women to search our souls and search the Bible. Oral and I did a lot of praying and discussing in those days after Australia. We appreciated even more the people who made commitments to the

Lord while we were there.

And you know, even out of this bad experience, the Lord worked miracles. Once we were gone, some of the press people came out for us and for God. One radio commentator related to his listeners the fact that we (Americans) had to leave the country because of hecklers. And he said he was ashamed of his fellow Australians. He asked the question, "Do we have religious freedom here or not?" So perhaps a seed of equivalent benefit was planted.

Nine years later, Oral went back to Australia. The questions were all there in my mind:

What will happen this time? Will we see any results from our crusades in Sydney and Melbourne? What will the press do against Oral this visit?

Well, the first few minutes there, a cab driver said, "Brother Roberts, I was converted to Christ in your crusade here nine years ago. God really picked me up from the gutter. I was an alcoholic and virtually bankrupt. I came to the meetings out of curiosity and there my entire family was saved. Now I am prospering and in nine years I've not wanted a drink. I've not missed a church service and I am daily witnessing for my Lord."

It was like that for three days — good report after good report — and God really blessed Oral's time with the Australian pastors and over 700 of the partners (Christians who supported us with their prayers).

Today, Australian stations still carry our radio broadcast and we have an overseas office in Australia. The manager of the Australian office sent us a report several years ago:

"Whether in the great cities or on the isolated aboriginal reserves, we are constantly finding lives that have been transformed and are meeting people who have been miraculously healed through your ministry here."

Over the years, I've reached two conclusions about controversies:

The first is never to respond in the spirit of accusation. Anger and resentment come from people who are bitter or who are experiencing unrest in their souls. To respond in that same way only makes things worse.

Oral's mother taught me that lesson. I never heard Mama Roberts criticize anyone. If she heard somebody else criticizing a person, she'd always say, "Watch *yourself,* and don't pay attention to what the other person is doing."

I said to her once, "You never say anything about anybody else. Why?"

And she said, "Why, Evelyn, I have such a hard time keeping *myself* in line! I have to use all the time I have to keep myself right with the Lord. I don't have any time to criticize anybody else."

Oral feels the same way. He doesn't criticize people, regardless of what they say to him or write about him. He never replies in a negative way.

The second conclusion is that it really doesn't matter what people say about you if you live right and do what the Lord tells you to do. In my heart I say to scoffers, "Who are you? What have you accomplished for God in your life?" I still want to put on my fighting clothes when people crtiticize my husband, but in the final account, I know that God's opinion will be the only one that counts. I've learned to believe in Romans 8:28:

*All things work together for good
to them that love God,
To them that are called according to
His purpose.*

Rebecca and Ronnie and Oral — A New Understanding

Rebecca and Ronnie, our eldest children, bore the brunt of the worst criticism leveled against Oral. By the time Richard and Roberta were in school, Oral was receiving less hostile press coverage.

Rebecca and Ronnie knew what "persecution" meant. Children at school would read newspaper articles about Oral and taunt them. Rebecca and Ronnie found themselves defending their dad because they knew the truth, but at the same time they resented the fact that their dad *needed* defense. They wanted a dad whom everybody respected — whom everybody thought was a great guy. Rebecca said to me one time, "I'll be so glad when I get old enough to be married and change my name from Roberts, because I will never have to bear again what I have gone through."

I said to Rebecca, "Well, just remember that you'll still be our daughter even when you have another name."

After Rebecca finished school, she began working in her dad's office. Some of her friends and acquaintances made slighting remarks about her not having any ability and that was the reason her dad hired her. After a couple of years of that, Rebecca felt she had to prove to herself and everybody else that she did have ability. Without saying anything to anybody, she went downtown to an insurance company and applied for a job. During the interview, she had to indicate past work experience. She didn't mind telling them she had worked at our office because a lot of people did — five hundred as a matter of fact. When the interview was over, the man said, "You're Oral Roberts's daughter, aren't you?"

That nearly killed Rebecca. She said, "Well, yes, but how did you *know* that?"

"Well, there is just something about you that's like your father," he said. "You seem very efficient and I'm hiring you today."

She took the job, but she realized in the process that she could never get away from the fact that she was Oral Roberts's daughter.

It's still that way for her, and it always will be, but she can laugh about it now. One day she joked with me, "Well, I was Oral Roberts's daughter, and then I was Marshall's wife, and now I'm Brenda's mommy! I guess I never will be my own person."

Ronnie, though, knew from the beginning he was stuck with the last name "Roberts." He not only had to deal with his dad's reputation, he had to actively seek his own identity. Ronnie was determined not to be judged by what his dad did or did not do. He was his own man and wanted others to recognize him as Ronald Roberts, *not* as "Oral Roberts's son."

I'm sure Ronnie was never ashamed of his father — he simply wanted to leave his own mark on people and not be prejudged.

As a child, Ronnie dearly loved the crusades. He'd sit on the platform when Oral prayed for the sick, and he thoroughly enjoyed it.

Sometimes I would say to Ronnie, "Now you need to be with your father."

And I would say to Oral, "You need to take Ronnie along with you. What difference does it make if he misses a few days of school."

Ronnie was eager to go, but he also got very bored during the days. He has an active mind, like Oral's, and if he isn't busy every minute, he gets bored. During the day, when Oral was preparing for the meeting that night — resting, studying his Bible, praying — Ronnie didn't have anybody to be with. He liked to be where the action was and take an active part. He was always willing to participate.

When Oral was a pastor and gave the altar call in churches, he always had Ronnie sing "Don't Turn Him Away." He had such a sweet little voice. I played the piano and Ronnie stood with his hand on the altar rail, singing. For some reason this always melted the hearts of people.

Ronnie began learning the Scriptures when he was about three years old. Oral would put him on his knee, while I cooked dinner, and have Ronnie repeat Scriptures after him. He memorized the Lord's Prayer, Psalm 23, Psalm 91, the first Psalm, and many more.

When he was about four, he'd stand in the back seat of the car behind his dad after the meetings and Oral would say "Ronnie, what did I preach about tonight?" And Ronnie would repeat the sermon almost verbatim. He has a mind that doesn't miss a thing and he could repeat his dad's sermons from the beginning to the end.

Ronnie loved to pray, too. When he was five years old, he was sleeping with his grandmother one night. She had a bad cough. It was a chronic cough that was a nuisance. Every time she went to bed she coughed for several minutes before she could go to sleep. This night, Ronnie became upset because of his granny's coughing and said, "Granny, let me pray for you."

She said, "All right, son."

He placed his hand on her head and prayed a childish prayer. She stopped coughing and rested well the rest of the night.

As Ronnie grew older, he found himself thoroughly enjoying sitting down with people and explaining the Bible to them. He would find himself in long conversations with people and they would be fascinated by him because they had never met anyone his age who knew so much about the Bible.

So — one side of Ronnie wanted everything his dad stood for. He believed in things Oral preached and in many ways he was like Oral. But the other side of Ronnie rebelled against the hurt, the persecution, and the constant defending of his dad. To compound the problem, he grew to resent the time Oral was away. He felt he didn't have his dad's time during his growing-up years when he needed him most.

I don't think there ever was a time when Oral would not have spent more time with Ronnie if he had known how Ronnie felt, but they never could seem to communicate with each other about this. Ronnie needed Oral's presence and his example to help him find his answers and his own identity. He felt cheated when he didn't have it.

I always felt that I had to be the go-between. My job was to keep peace among the children, and keep peace between the children and their dad. I never wanted any animosity to appear in our family. But, as Ronnie became a teen-ager and left for college, the animosity was plainly there and it grew. It got to the point where he felt completely alienated.

When he went to Stanford University, he felt that was the ideal time to get away from all the persecution. It was a jolt to realize that even 1,500 miles away he could not escape the fact that his name was Roberts — and the moment somebody asked him his name and then where he was from, they would associate him with his dad. Professors ridiculed him as Oral Roberts's son. College became the opposite of what Ronnie had expected.

Finally, the hurting and the inner conflict came to a climax. Ronnie came home for a long weekend with us and the hurt spilled out. We had long talks and long prayers together that weekend. Ronnie got out of his system all of the things he wanted to say to his dad, and his dad did the same.

Ronnie said, ''Dad, I felt I was denied

your time and your concentration in my growing-up years. I desperately needed you. I needed to get your views on certain things and you were always gone. When I had a question, you weren't around to answer it. When you came home, you were tired from the crusade and we tried not to disturb you. I had to learn to live with many of my fears. I wanted to know if you really were a fraud like everybody said. I wanted to know if the Bible was right or if people were right in telling me that there was nothing true in the Bible. I couldn't ask you these questions and something developed in me that I don't like. I feel you weren't with me those years, and I *resent* it. I resent the fact that the people had you when I didn't.''

And Oral said to him, ''Ronnie, I know that. Your mother and I have talked about this many times. But if I had to do it again, I *could not* change what I did because I have to obey the Lord, regardless of family or whomever. I *have* to do what God says to do. I've questioned myself and I've questioned God many times. 'Lord, my children are at home and I'm out here trying to win other people's children to you — *what about my own?*' But the Lord never released me, Ronnie. God was calling me and I couldn't go back on God's call. I'm sorry I didn't spend more time with you, but I hope that I can make it up to you some way, or that the Lord will make it up to you. Maybe when your children are growing up, you will realize some of the things that I've gone through. I think there will be a time when you'll understand."

Soon after this, Ronnie quit Stanford and joined the army. He was sent to Fort Ord, California, because he requested language school. He had been a foreign-exchange student while in high school and had spent one summer studying in Formosa. (He speaks German, French, Chinese, and several other languages fluently.) So he was assigned to study Polish at the army school in Monterey, California. While he was stationed there, we received a telephone call from him saying that he had a serious case of hepatitis and was in the isolation ward of the military hospital at Fort Ord. We flew out to be with him and found him yellow with jaundice and so thin it broke my heart. Ron was not only sick in his body; there was also something wrong in his spirit — his inner person. After his doctor told us it would be four months before Ronnie could be released, we asked for a private room and took him in with us. I said to him, "Ronnie, if God gets on this case, it need not be four months. Do you believe that, Ronnie?"

He said, "Yes, I do, Mother."

Oral took him in his arms and commanded Satan to loose our son. I remember that he said, "Devil, take your hands off God's property. You shall not have our son — neither his body, his soul, nor his mind."

Then we asked Jesus to take charge and heal him completely. Ronnie was visibly shaken — God did something special for him that day. Not only was he healed physically but wounds were healed that had been there a long time. Four weeks later he called us to report he was being dismissed from the hospital.

That was the beginning of a healing between Ronnie and Oral. Many conversations and much prayer, coupled with maturity in Ronnie and age in Oral, have softened their hearts toward each other, and they found that they are really on the same wave length. In fact, I tell Ronnie, sometimes, that when I'm in another room and hear the two of them talking, I am amazed at how much he is like his father. They both have analytical minds and they ask "why" about everything. They have to get to the bottom of things.

In no way is Ronnie more like his dad than when he prays. Some time ago, Oral was very ill. We had prayed but there still was no relief from the pain. He was under a doctor's care but the medicine wasn't working. Finally, Oral said to me, "Get Ronnie on the phone." When I did, Oral came to the phone and he broke down started to cry. And he said, "Ronnie, your mother has prayed for me, our friends have prayed for me, but I've got to have a prayer from you."

Ronnie has a tone of authority in his voice like his dad. And he commands the sickness to leave exactly like Oral does. Oral couldn't stop weeping, but I heard him say, "Oh, yes, Ronnie, I'm going to be all right. I'm going to get well from this moment."

Ronnie told me that he had said, "Now, Dad, I'm going to be believing with you that the Lord did something for you."

And Oral had said, "I know He did. I'm going to go and get dressed right now because from this moment I'm going to be well." And he did!

Four years ago Ronnie moved his family to Tulsa after having been away twelve years. He and his father are having some marvelous times of talk and relaxation together. They're really getting to know each other, and I have watched the appreciation they have for each other grow day by day.

When I hear the two of them talk about life, the Bible, God in the now, and what God is to people, they sound the same — and yet Ronnie has reached most of his opinions through his own searching and studying.

Ronnie is currently finishing a doctorate in linguistics and is teaching literature in Tulsa. He has said, "Dad, when I say something to you, it's my own idea. I'm not parroting anything that anyone else has ever said to me. I am an independent thinker and I come to my own conclusions. I listen to people, and I listen to you. But your views are not necessarily my views. When I tell you something, it comes out of my own thinking because I study the Bible a great deal. The Bible is the greatest piece of literature ever written and I include it in my teaching of literature because it's a great book. But I also give the Bible to my students for its content.''

Rebecca and Ronnie have matured because of their persecution — and I'm grateful that they are as strong in their inner spirits as they are today. But as a mother, I am *most* grateful that we are a unified family.

Not that Ronnie was the only child with whom we had a serious misunderstanding! There was Richard!

Richard and Patti

People ask, "Can a mother and father choose their children's calling?" I believe parents can discern, *through prayer,* if their children will be used to spread the gospel in some way. When my children were small, I prayed that God would call at least one of them to be a missionary. I suppose it was because I had wanted to be a called missionary. One tends to live his own dreams through his children.

At that time I thought a missionary was a person who went overseas to work for a lifetime and came home only on furlough. Today, I think Richard is as much a missionary as anyone ever has been. He's rarely been overseas to minister, but the role of a missionary has changed. It is true that Jesus said, *"Go ye into all the world and preach the gospel to every creature."* but as Oral so often points out, that also means going into every person's world. I believe my prayer has been answered.

Ten years ago, I never could have said that, and I probably wouldn't have thought it. Richard was the rebel in our family — not only rebellious against Oral and me, but rebellious against God.

There was a difference in the rebellion of Ronnie and Richard. Richard was very open. He'd say right to Oral's face, "Dad, get off my back. Let me alone. I'll have none of this."

Or he would come to me and say, "Now, Mother, let me tell you something. I'm not going to put up with Dad much longer." Richard was out in the open with his grievances. I think the person who can get his problems out in the open gets along better. He may hurt a lot of people with what he says, but the problems never have the chance to fester inside. Richard's was an open rebellion, and he didn't care who knew it.

Many times we asked Richard not to go to some of the places he frequented when he was in high school. He didn't say he would or wouldn't. He just left, and went. He never sassed me. I'd never stand for that. But he'd quietly walk out and do just as he pleased without uttering a word.

When he was in high school, he was ill one day and stayed home in bed. Oral and I felt he was struggling with something in his mind. I believe God was dealing with him. We both went into his room to pray with him, and his dad had a vision as we prayed.

When we finished praying, Oral said, "Richard, I could see you. There was a great lake and you were trying to wade into the water, but you were wading right at the edge. There was much deep water that you had to go through to get to where I was." And he added, "Richard, I fear for you, because you and I are the same. When there is a call of God on your life as you have and as I have, there's no way to get around it. Some people can go through life and dillydally around, but you're not one of them and neither am I."

Even this didn't fully sober Richard, although I'm sure he must have thought about it many times. He wanted to live his own life and make his own decisions — without regard for God's will in his life.

One thing Richard did *not* want to do was attend Oral Roberts University. He didn't want to go to a school where his dad was president and he also had some habits that ORU would not allow. He smoked and did a lot of other things while singing in some coffeehouses and nightclubs. He plainly wasn't a prospective ORU student. He could hardly wait to get away from home and off to college.

Oral was kind of "put down" by Richard's decision. He said to me, "I've built a university and my own son doesn't even want to come."

And I believe Oral might have tried to force Richard to attend, but I said to him, "Now, Oral, you cannot force a child to go to a college. You can guide him and tell him what you think, but if you force him to go to ORU, he will never be a good student and he will be wasting his time. Naturally, we would like for him to attend ORU, but I think he'll get along better if you just tell the Lord about it and let the Lord handle Richard."

Oral finally agreed, and Richard chose Kansas University. We did a lot of praying in those days for the Lord to guide Richard in the way *He* wanted him to go.

Richard's letters revealed that he wasn't really happy at KU that first year. First of all there were 17,000 students there, and he felt lost in the maze. In one letter he said he felt as if he was just a number instead of a person. By no means am I implying that all students feel the way Richard did at a big school. His unhappiness said to me that God was trying to get him headed in the right direction and that ORU was part of God's plan for him.

When God has a plan for you and you're not in it, then whatever you're doing doesn't seem to be right, and you have all kinds of problems until you get back on the path that God wants you to walk. Richard was gifted in a way that could help us in our ministry. God knew this and we knew this.

The last thing Richard wanted was to be a part of Oral's ministry. That was one of the reasons he was eager to get away from home. He had no desire to sing in his dad's crusades, none whatsoever. And yet, when he was five years old, we had stood him in a chair at a crusade in Maryland and he sang "I Believe" before 10,000 people. Not only did we know what he could do, Satan knew.

During the spring term, toward the end of school, Richard came home for a weekend and I could tell he had really enjoyed being home. When he returned to school he called and said, "Mother, I've been thinking that I'd like to come to ORU next year."

"Richard, I don't believe you'll be accepted by ORU because you have some habits that ORU will not accept. And unless you make a major change in your life, ORU will not accept you even though you are the president's son. We won't make an exception even for you."

"Well, I can change."

"Yes, and you will have to."

"Well, we'll see about it, Mother. If I don't come to ORU, would you consider letting me get an apartment at KU and live off campus?"

"Never."

Oral and I had allowed Ronnie to get an apartment and live off campus, which we later realized was a mistake. I didn't intend to make that mistake again.

Richard came to look over ORU that summer during a seminar and one of the professors was assigned to be his adviser. I don't know what he told that man and I don't know what that professor told Richard, but it must have been something good because Richard was impressed that he had received the right advice. And he suddenly decided it was time that he made a change in his life and that he'd come to ORU in the right way.

For the first time, Richard was willing to go with his dad and sing in the crusades. He went to a few meetings in the Dayton, Ohio, crusade and that is where he made the first adult commitment of his life. He changed his habits and he changed his mind about God and his father's ministry.

Richard thought he had made a *total* commitment of his life. He didn't realize he hadn't until he and Patti Holcombe, an ORU student, began to talk seriously about getting married. Patti was a talented musician and a member of the ORU Collegians, later the World Action Singers. I think Richard was attracted by her talent, but was captivated by her deep Christian commitment and her warm, loving personality. They fell in love and planned to be married.

Several weeks before the wedding, Oral and I were in California for a crusade, and at the end of the meetings Oral suggested we stay in California for a couple of days and rest.

I said, "Oral, I have to go home."

"Why? Our children are grown. They can take care of themselves. You can call and see if Richard and Roberta are all right."

"I know I could, Oral, but I just feel that for some reason I have to go home."

So I flew home on a Sunday afternoon and when I arrived, nobody was at the house. Richard was living on campus and Roberta was away. After I brought in my suitcases, I picked up the Sunday paper and sat down for a moment. Then I heard the back door slam. I knew it had to be Richard. Nobody slams the door quite like

Richard, except his dad, and I knew his dad was in California. He said, "Mother, I'm so glad you came home because I am in real trouble."

"What's your trouble, Richard?"

I thought to myself, "Well, now I'll find out why I was supposed to come home." I could just imagine Richard breaking a rule and being expelled.

"I'm in real trouble. I cannot make Patti believe that I really love her."

"Well, Richard, what have you done to make her feel that you don't love her?"

"I haven't done anything, Mother. I haven't done anything, but she just suddenly said to me, 'Richard, I don't feel that you love me enough to get married, so let's just call the whole thing off.' "

"Well, how do you feel about that?"

"I'm just wiped out, Mother. I do love her. I love her so much I just can't be without her and I just have to have her — that's all. I'm lost without her."

I began to feel that I knew what Patti meant. Patti was feeling that Richard had not really made a *total* commitment to the Lord.

"Richard," I said, "when you made a commitment of your life to the Lord, did you make a one-sided commitment? Did you say, 'Lord, I'll do anything for You if You'll just give me Patti.'?"

He looked directly at me.

"Richard, if that's the kind of commitment you made, it's not the right kind. When you make a commitment to the Lord, you promise to serve Him regardless of what happens, Patti or no Patti. Richard, you can live without Patti, whether you think you can or not. But you can't live without the Lord. You are going to have to know — beyond a shadow of a doubt — that the Lord is first in your life."

I could tell I was really getting to him. "Why don't we just pray about it?"

I'll never forget that moment. Richard sank to his knees and put his head on my lap, just as he had as a little boy, and he cried as if his heart would break. He began telling the Lord, "Lord, I'll serve You — Patti or not." And then he'd stop, and I could tell he didn't want to give up Patti. But he was telling the Lord, "Lord, I will.

This time I really mean it, Lord. I'll really do it. If you don't want me to have Patti, it's all right. I'll serve You whether I get Patti or not."

It was hard for him to say. Oh, it was hard. But I knew when the joy came and he had really made up his mind because his hands just automatically went up in the air, and he began praising the Lord.

I had not heard Richard use his prayer language since he was about twelve. Suddenly he began praising the Lord in the prayer language of the Spirit. And then, of course, we were both praising the Lord. I knew the joy had come and I knew the commitment had been made and everything would be all right.

Richard told me later that he had wanted so much to go to Patti that night and tell her he had made a big change in his life, but he said, "I didn't. Something just kind of held me back. When I got back to the dorm and went to my room, four or five guys were in my room on their knees praying. I realized they were praying for me. They were praying that I would make a complete commitment of my life to the

Lord because they knew, too, that I hadn't. I joined them and said, 'Guys, you're too late, I've already done it.' And we *really* had a prayer meeting."

The next day, when Richard went to class, he saw Patti and started to tell her what had happened. She looked at him and said, "Richard, everything is okay. I prayed about it last night, and God gave me a green light."

And Richard said, "Oh, Mother, my heart sang all day. I went around with a song in my heart all day."

Then he called Oral in California and said, "Dad, everything is okay now. I want to do what I can to help you in your ministry."

That was the beginning of a new Richard. Richard and Patti were married a few weeks later. They began to appear with the World Action Singers and are now regular and active participants in all aspects of the television ministry. They often travel with us when Oral addresses a large group of people. While Oral is still chairman of the board, Richard was recently elected by the trustees as president of the Oral

Roberts Association.

Moreover, Richard and Patti appear in their own gospel concerts and have their own musical ministry. I'll never forget their concert in Dallas in 1973. That was the first time Oral and I had ever been to a concert when they were entirely on their own. The Lord's anointing was so great on their singing that people in the packed auditorium wept throughout the concert and it was a great experience for Oral and me — to know this program was theirs and that the anointing of the Lord was on their lives. I saw my son and daughter-in-law as ministers in their own right — as missionaries to a generation of young people who need to hear more about God's love.

Learning to Let Go

My husband worked very hard, from the time our children were tiny, to help me begin to give them up. He often said to me, "The more you are gone from your children, the more independent they become. We're trying to raise these children to be independent citizens. They must learn to live on their own. They must not hold our skirts when they're adults."

It was my nature to cling to my children. It was harder for me to give up my girls than it was to give up my boys. I don't know why.

Rebecca married when she was nineteen. I promised her I would not cry and spoil her wedding. She had a beautiful garden wedding on the first of June. We had a white picket fence with roses entwined with a gatelike arch where she and Marshall stood to repeat their vows. She was beautiful and happy and I enjoyed doing things for her.

It rained for days before the wedding. The day arrived and clouds still covered the sun. Someone remarked, "Surely Oral has asked the Lord about having sunshine. If he will ask, I believe the Lord will intervene." (Oral always has a reply to that. He says "I'm in sales, not management.")

The household was all astir. We thought we might have to have the wedding indoors. But by noon the clouds were edged with gold and by the time the guests began to arrive, the sun was shining. Rebecca was a beautiful bride as she marched with her father down the grassy carpet to stand under the arch. There she took the hand of Marshall Nash and the minister spoke the words that gave her entrance to a new world of love and happiness.

Oral had first declared that he would not walk down the aisle and give his daughter to anyone, but I persisted for Rebecca's sake and he consented.

He had told Rebecca from the time she was thirteen or fourteen that if she would elope, he'd help her and that would save an expensive wedding! Every time I said something to Rebecca about dreading the time she'd get married and leave home, Oral would speak up and say, "Well, I want her to get married."

When the minister asked, "Who giveth this girl?" Oral answered, "I do"; and when he turned to be seated, the pained look on his face showed his true feeling. She was no longer our little girl, dependent on us. She was now a woman — able to think for herself. He had held her on his knee and taught her about Jesus. He had watched her grow up happy and carefree. And now the firstborn was leaving the nest.

When the guests had gone and the happy couple had left for their honeymoon, Oral looked at me and said, "Don't ever ask me to give another one of my children away because I won't do it."

By the time the reception was over, I was so exhausted I went straight to sleep. Early in the morning I awoke, and suddenly the fact hit me, "She's gone. She's really gone. Where are those nineteen short years?" The tears began to roll and I sobbed.

Oral awoke and said, "Evelyn, what is it?"

"Oh, Oral, Rebecca will never be back here to live."

That's when I learned to *start* letting go. Little by little, incidents arose that taught me to let go more and more.

I learned an important lesson right after Rebecca first married. She and Marshall planned a trip to Georgia with a man who owned his own small airplane. It had only one engine. It scared me half to death when I learned that they were going in this plane with just one engine.

"Oh, Rebecca," I said. "I don't want you to go in that plane. I don't think it's safe and I just don't think you all ought to go." I put in my two cents' worth when I should have kept my mouth shut. And, as a result, I ruined the entire trip. Marshall went without Rebecca.

Rebecca told me later, "Mother, it was the most miserable weekend I ever spent. I would rather have gone with my husband and died than to have stayed at home alone. I cried the whole weekend."

I learned, then, that when my children

marry, I must quit ordering their lives. They aren't clinging to me anymore and I must give them up. It's for their sakes as well as mine. And I learned that I couldn't tear myself up with the way I might feel about their goings and comings.

I felt I had to go to Rebecca and say, "Rebecca, I apologize for this because I realize I made a mistake, and I hope the Lord will help me never to say a word about what you do. You're not at home anymore. I'm not responsible for you. You're living with a husband and you have the right to go anywhere you want to go and do anything you want to do. Please don't tell me about your trips from now on. Just go. Don't ask me or tell me." I learned a great lesson from that.

I think the only time that Rebecca and Oral ever had a serious clash was when Rebecca was working for us at the office. After she was married, and while we were in California one summer, she bleached her naturally black hair *blond*.

Oral had to come home for a few days and he called Rebecca and asked her to meet him at the airport. Well, when he got off the plane, he didn't even recognize her. When he realized that the blonde was Rebecca, he came as near to having a heart attack as he has ever come in his entire life. As the young people say now, "it wiped him out." And not only that — but Ronnie was standing beside her with a goatee!

His daughter with blond hair and his son with a beard! He said to me later, "If I had died right there, I wouldn't have been surprised. To see that beautiful black hair ruined, and Ronnie with that beard, it just did me in."

He was so shocked he didn't know what to say. He called me that night and said, "If Rebecca was not an employee in our office, I wouldn't say anything to her, as much as I'm disappointed. But, Evelyn, I can't have her setting a trend in the office. People who dye and bleach their hair aren't well respected." (Remember, this was 1960!)

Well, Oral prayed about it that night and then he called Rebecca into his office the next day. He said, "Now, Rebecca, you are married, and if you were not my employee, I would have nothing to say about your hair. But you *are* an employee, and as long as I'm paying you, I have a right to tell you what I think. And I think you should get your purse and go home and not come back to work until your hair is its natural color. I'm sorry I have to tell you this.''

Well, it was a real break between Rebecca and her daddy and it was a long time before she got over it. She thought it was none of her dad's business because she was married, but she didn't say a word to Oral.

She talked to Ronnie about it, but she never mentioned it to me. Marshall said to her, ''Well, there is one thing I want you to do before you dye your hair back. I want a picture of you.'' So, he has one picture of Rebecca as a blonde.

Finding a balance between letting go and learning to relate to our children as adults wasn't easy for any of us.

Roberta — My Baby

Just as there is something special about a very first baby, there is also something very special about a last child.

When Roberta came to us we had had two boys in a row and Rebecca was fed up with brothers who pestered her. She said to me as I went to the hospital, "Mother, if this baby is a boy, I'm going to leave home."

Not only was she not a boy, but she was very beautiful, petite, little girl — so feminine, so doll-like, all of us fell in love with her at first sight.

She and Richard were two years apart and even though he pestered her when they were growing up, he always protected her.

In many ways Roberta is like her father, and Ronnie — a student always and forever, but a very sensitive person. She is easily hurt, especially by those closest to her.

She always seemed to need more love and affection in her growing-up years and required more attention. I remember once when Oral was away at a crusade he called us as he often did when he was away. He always talked to each of the children. It seemed to make all of us feel closer together.

On this particular call, we had all finished and were telling each other what Daddy said. I said to Roberta, who was about three, "What did Daddy say to you, Honey?"

She just shrugged her little shoulders and said, "Oh, he *uves* me."

Oral and I spent more time at her bedside than any of the others simply because she would announce to all of us, "I'm going to bed. No one in this house loves me." I'm glad we recognized her need for our attention because each time after prayer and much conversation the need seemed to diminish.

Her sensitive nature is probably partly responsible for her deep spiritual

226

commitment. Having accepted Jesus into her heart at an early age, Roberta was really never rebellious. Of our four children, I believe Roberta loved the crusades the most.

As a teen-ager, she traveled for several years with her dad during the summers and played the organ. Roberta has taken organ and piano lessons nearly all her life and has a beautiful talent. I remember once, during high school, she was about to give up her lessons and I was distressed. So I said, "Oral, you must talk to Roberta. She'll be sorry some day if she stops her lessons because she's so good and a talent like hers should be used."

So Oral called her in one night and shared with her the parable about the ten talents from the Bible (Matthew 25). Oral encouraged her to develop her abilities and use them for the Lord. Roberta still plays for the seminars occasionally and is a fine organist and pianist.

Even though she is very much like her father, she and I are close, so much that I was rather shocked when she wanted to take a tour of Europe. I couldn't make up my mind that she could get along without me, but I learned that even babies grow up.

It hit me hard when I watched her go down the aisle to become Mrs. Ronald Potts — my baby girl, my last child — flown from my protecting arms.

I wanted Roberta and Ron to wait until they graduated before they married. They were both attending ORU, but they didn't listen, as most children don't listen.

However, it was a proud moment for Oral and me when we saw her at graduation with her cap and gown and heard Dr. Hamilton say, "Roberta Roberts Potts," as she went to receive her degree. Dean Hamilton asked me to come up and place the hood on her shoulders. How thrilled I was to have one of our children reap some of the benefits of our labors at ORU.

She is an administrative assistant in a responsible position now — and a proud wife and mother.

Money

When Oral is faced with a tough decision that must be made, he always asks himself, "What does God want me to do?" The first question that comes to *my* mind is, "How much will it cost?"

I think about money — and money seems to be a major concern when *other* people think about Oral's ministry — but money isn't a concern to Oral. He cares only about doing the right thing in the right way: excellently and honestly.

I can think of nothing worse than a dishonest preacher. Unpaid debts are a bad mark on a ministry, on a denomination, and on a church. Dishonesty can destroy a person.

One morning during our Enid pastorate, Oral hit the fender of our neighbor's car while backing out of the driveway. The car was parked in the street and he could easily have driven on and never told the neighbor. But he stopped the car, went to the door, and said, "Sir, I'm Oral Roberts. I live next door and I'm the pastor of a little church here. I just backed out and hit your car. I want you to tell me how much the damages come to when you have your car fixed, and I'll take care of the bill."

The man said, "Well, Mr. Roberts, why didn't you just go on and not tell me about it? I never would have known who did it."

And Oral said, "No, but *I* would have known."

Once in California, Oral was playing golf at a country club and his golf ball hit a luxury car parked near the clubhouse. It made quite a dent! So, off went Oral, searching for the owner of the car, but with no luck. By the time he got back, the car was gone. He did learn the man's name and he called him at home and said, "Sir, my name is Oral Roberts. I want you to know my golf ball hit your car and when you get the car fixed, I want you to send me the bill so I can pay for the repairs."

The man said, "Are you the Oral Roberts

on television?"

"Yes, sir."

"Well, Mr. Roberts, why did you call me about this?"

"Because I hit your car and I want to pay for the damage."

"You didn't have to tell me. I never would have known you did it."

And Oral said, "Yes, but *I* would have known."

A month or so later the man sent us the bill, and after Oral sent the money to him, he received a beautiful letter. I don't believe the man really thought Oral meant what he said and he sent us the bill to see if we were honest. He didn't need the money because we found out later he was a member of one of the wealthiest families in the United States. And *we* surely could have used the money. But it was a debt owed, so it was a debt we paid.

As a young pastor, Oral had a great fund of creative energy. He was restless, and out of his restlessness he sought new ways to reach people for God. He had more ideas than fifty average people. Almost all of them were good. Some worked. Some he didn't have a chance to try because he didn't have the money to test them.

It wasn't uncommon for him to use our grocery money to help accomplish some pet project for God. When he got a new idea, he was always eager to test it. It didn't seem to bother him, as it sometimes irritated me, if it took all the money we had.

One day he came home with a bright idea. World War II was at its height. Oral had tried to enlist as a chaplain, but he wasn't accepted because he lacked the required number of college hours. He felt he should do *something,* so he wrote a pamphlet directed to the soldier about how to know Jesus and serve Him as Lord. The printer's bill alone was sixty-five dollars. It took all our savings to pay it. And do you think Oral would sell the pamphlets to pay for the cost of printing? No. He *gave* them all away. When I reproached him, his reply was, "Someday the Lord is going to let me do what I *want* to do for the people. And I won't have to worry about money."

How ashamed I was! My thrifty German ancestry was caught showing.

When Oral began his crusade ministry, he

made a vow to God that he would touch neither *the gold nor the glory.*

By "glory" he meant he wanted to give God the praise for every miracle. And I personally think he's been scrupulously honest and sincere in doing just that. He has always told people, *"I* cannot heal you. Only God can heal." Some people have called him a "faith healer," saying that Oral Roberts heals or that he claims to heal. But Oral and I both know — and he would tell you himself — that *he* has never healed anybody. Only God heals.

Oral feels that God has given him a gift to *help* people with their faith. He believes if he can inspire a person to release his faith, and in so doing be healed by God — physically, mentally, or spiritually — then he is doing what God called him to do. He has never claimed a gift of healing. I know the Lord has worked through him, and does work through him, with healing power. But Oral believes that the gifts of God are *resident in God* and resident in Jesus — not resident in the person using them. He believes a gift flows through him at the time it is needed, and any one of the nine spiritual gifts in the Bible can flow through *any* Spirit-filled Christian. As far as Oral is concerned, *any* Christian can do what he has done and is doing, if he will yield his life to the Lord.

I never have agreed with him on this. I believe Oral is a "specially-called" person for a special work. One of the ways God uses him is in casting demons out of people. Twice in my life I have proven that *I* certainly don't have that gift.

During one of the early Sunday-afternoon services we had while still in Enid, a strange woman came to our service. Many people in the community felt she was demon-possessed. Her actions were not normal. On this particular Sunday, Oral went over to pray for her.

I thought, "Well, I'm his helper and I'm supposed to help him, so I'll just walk over there with him." But learned quickly it was no place for me. As we approached her, she struck out with her hands and shoved me back. She didn't even touch Oral. He prayed for her and she became calm. I realized then God had given him a special gift that I did not have.

On another occasion I was praying alone with a lady. I didn't realize she was demon-possessed until the spirits in her began to hiss at me. I told the woman, "I can only pray for you and leave it up to the Spirit of God to deliver you. The Lord has not given me power over demons in the way that he has given it to my husband. I do not feel this is my gift, and I don't believe a person can deal with demons unless the Lord has given him a special gift. I think it's dangerous."

Another reason that I feel Oral has special gifts — or he has let special gifts flow through him — is that so many, many people have been healed through his ministry. However, to him, the fact that he possesses gifts or abilities is not important. The important thing is that people are in need and God is the source of their total supply. He will not touch the "glory" for miracles that happen around him.

When it comes to the "gold" — money — he never accepts personal gifts in exchange for prayer. His prayers are not for sale. They never have been. I have seen people try to put money in his hands after he has prayed for them, and he always says, "I can't take it. God might remove His gifts from me."

These people are not necessarily trying to buy healing, nor are they trying to "pay" him. They just want to give out of the kindness of their hearts.

"Oh, Brother Roberts, I'm not trying to *pay* you," they say, "I just want to give you this."

He always replies, "If you want to give it for the *ministry,* then give it to someone else and let him put it into the ministry offering. But don't give it to me because I won't touch it. I promised the Lord that I would not touch *gold* for praying for people."

As far as the money that comes in for the ministry is concerned, we are scrupulously honest. So many dishonest evangelists have traveled around the country that we have had to be scrupulous. We had to live down their reputations.

In most places where we went for crusades, city ordinances required that a person have a permit to raise a tent. The fire inspector had to come and inspect the tent. In some places, the seats had to be wired together. We bent backward to comply with these laws.

One evangelist made it a practice of going from city to city, putting up his tent without a permit. Big headlines would tell how the city ran him out of town. People would say, "These evangelists come through the town and think they can defy the city officials. They put up their tents, have their meetings, promise people things they can never deliver, and take our money. We don't want any more charlatan faith healers coming into town to put up tents." And that made it hard on us because the next line would be, "And isn't Oral Roberts just like all the rest of them?" No, he wasn't, and we had to live down those things.

In those crusade days, a love offering was taken for us one night during the crusade. We didn't receive a salary from any group of people. We believed that as people were blessed, they would help us meet our financial needs. The love offering was announced at the beginning of each crusade: "There will be only one love offering taken for Brother Roberts during these meetings. If you want to give to help meet his personal expenses, come prepared on a certain night. All of the other offerings go for the expenses of the crusade." So everybody knew in advance. It was an established fact. The Bureau of Internal Revenue (now Internal Revenue Service) knew it. Our auditor knew it. Our attorneys knew it. In fact, one of the auditors came to the crusades and helped count the Friday-night offering so it could be accurately reported to the Bureau of Internal Revenue.

As we gave of our lives to people, we found they gave back to us. We were never wealthy but we always had enough. We spent our money wisely and made some investments in land or property.

I have never been able to understand why many people don't want their pastors and ministers to live as well as they do. Some people seem to feel that preachers have to be poor to be sincere. To me preaching is a profession, a profession which demands a call from God. It is an honorable way of making a living.

We continued to rely on the love offering as the means of our personal support until about the late fifties. At that time, Oral felt directed to receive a set salary for his position as the president of the Oral Roberts Association. He wanted to give what we had saved to begin Oral Roberts University, but he felt, too, an obligation to our children who also had made a great sacrifice for the ministry. So, we took the land and real estate we had purchased and the cash in our savings account and divided it right down the middle — half going to Oral Roberts University and the other half into a trust fund for our children. After years of saving it's not easy to suddenly sink everything you have into a brand-new project, but the call of God to build a university was so strong, we had to do it. God gives Oral orders — not suggestions. Also, Oral wanted to leave a testimony that his ministry was not based on the size of his income. He wanted people to know that he did what he did because he loved God and people. This move limited our income, but we have been made increasingly aware that *God* is not limited, and for every seed planted, we are due a harvest.

Throughout his ministry, Oral has taught that when people give to God, their supply is not depleted. The Lord always gives us back everything we've ever given Him — *plus!* I love the Scripture Oral so often uses about the woman with the meal and oil, who had just enough to cook one little cake for herself and her son before they faced starvation (I Kings 17:10-16). When Elijah, the servant of God, came along, he said, "The Lord says for you to give me [God's servant] the first, and after that you'll have plenty." And she did.

We taught our children this principle. They grew up believing that the Lord doesn't *take* things away from people, but when you freely give to Him, He blesses you abundantly in return. We taught them to give a portion of their weekly allowances to the church. I never wanted my children to be stingy, especially with the Lord. They'd take their Sunday school money and give some in Sunday school and some in the offering plate during the church service. I shall never forget one Sunday coming home from church. Richard, about eight or nine, announced to us, "I gave 10 percent of my money to God today."

I said, "Richard, how much did you give?"

"Well, I gave a dollar and thirty-three cents."

"How much did you have?"

"I had three dollars."

He never could do much with arithmetic. But God has given back to him in the *measure* he gives (Luke 6:38).

Today, Oral receives a salary as president of Oral Roberts University. He receives *no* compensation for his work for the Oral Roberts Association. We live in a house built for the president of Oral Roberts University. We believe that, as His children, God wants us to enjoy the good things in life, but He also wants us to be prudent — never to let material things become more important than our love for Him.

I believe God wants *all* Christians to live an abundant life. I have a Scripture and an experience that tells me that. Read III John 2!

III John 2: The Scripture That Changed Our Lives

In 1947 Oral and I discovered a Scripture that literally changed our lives. It is a positive, uplifting Scripture that turned our concept of giving around from man's perspective to God's perspective. It is a Scripture that tells how God desires to take care of our needs and wants.

The Scripture is III John 2, which says:

Beloved, I wish above all things that you may prosper and be in health, even as your soul prospers.

To me, prosperity includes our wants as well as our needs. And I accept that as a promise to me from God. I think our desires are just as important to God as our needs.

God wants our material needs met. He

242

does not want us to be poverty stricken. He is just as concerned about our car payments, dental and medical bills, food bills, and rent as we are. He wants us to prosper.

God is concerned, too, about our health. He doesn't want us to be sick. He doesn't want our heads to ache, our ears to be deaf, our eyes to be blind, or our bodies to be crippled. Neither does He want us to be mentally broken.

And He is concerned about our souls — that spiritual part of us. He wants to have a personal relationship with each one of us for all eternity.

God's highest wish for us is that we be whole people.

Everything in this Scripture points to the fact that *God is a good God.* He is totally good and everything He does is good. He is the exact opposite of the devil.

The devil hates us and wants to deprive us of everything that is good or uplifting or that would bring joy into our lives. On the other hand, God loves us and wants to give us everything that brings life and an abundance of goodness.

When our children were little they heard

Oral say "God is a good God, and the devil is a bad devil" so often that I would overhear them saying it in their play.

In those days, many people didn't believe God was a good God. People often talked about God in a disparaging way. They felt if you missed a step, God would throw you into a hell without a trial. God turned out to be a greedy, harsh judge instead of a loving Being. People believed God wanted to *take* from man and give out punishment. But III John 2 says *exactly* the opposite. This Scripture is about giving and about a giving God who wants us to be on top, not at the bottom.

Here is how we discovered this Scripture in a very practical way.

We were living in Enid and Oral was attending Phillips University in addition to preaching. Every morning before he left to catch the bus, he would sit down in the living room, pick up his Bible, and read a portion of Scripture.

One morning he was in a hurry because he was late for class. He grabbed his books and ran out to catch the bus, but when he got to the bus, he remembered he hadn't read his Bible. So he came rushing back into the house and scooped up the Bible. He opened it to III John 2 and read, "I wish above all things that thou mayest prosper and be in health, even as thy soul prospereth."

He shouted excitedly, "Evelyn, come in here." When I went into the living room, Oral said, "Let me read you a verse of Scripture." And he read III John 2 to me.

"Oral, that's not in the Bible."

"It *is* in the Bible. I just read it."

"You've read the Bible a hundred times. If it *is* there, why haven't you found it before?"

We had been taught that Christians had to be poor. It was the mark of Christianity to have poverty on your side. We paid our tithes to the Lord faithfully. We never expected anything back. We believed as many people believe: What you give to God is gone.

I said, "Oral, it can't be. That Scripture is against everything we have been taught."

"I know it is, but it's here. I just read it."

He read it aloud — again, and again,

and again; and finally he said to me, "Evelyn, do you believe the Lord would give us a new car?"

I said, "No, Oral, I really don't." (I didn't have *that* much faith!)

"Well, *I* do, and I'm going to *believe* for it."

Finding that verse was really the beginning of our worldwide ministry. If we were to help people get their needs met, we had to know that God could meet ours.

A few days later, our next-door neighbor saw Oral mowing the lawn and he called across the fence, "Mr. Roberts, I am a car dealer and I've noticed that car of yours is getting pretty old and worn out."

Oral agreed, "You can say that again."

"Well, why not let me sell you a new one?"

"Sir, I can hardly keep up the payments on this one, much less buy a new one."

(And *that* was the truth. The phrase Oral sometimes used to describe his upbringing was true of us then — "We were so poor the poor people called us poor!")

The neighbor said, "Well, I'll tell you what we'll do. You sell this old car and get as much for it as you can. I go get new cars about every two weeks and bring them back, and I always take some people with me to help drive. How would you like to go with me and drive a car back, and we'll arrange the payments so you can afford a new car?''

When Oral came into the house and told me what had happened, it was as if the Lord had struck us with lightning. I couldn't believe what was happening. Oral said to me, ''See, I told you I was going to believe for a new car, didn't I?''

''Yes, and I told you I wasn't.''

''That's all right,'' he said. ''I don't care if you believe or not. *I* am believing for a new car and the Lord is going to give us one.''

Well, we drove up north with Mr. Gus, our neighbor, and picked up a brand-new, long, green Buick. As we drove out of town toward home, it suddenly hit me, ''This is a miracle. God has really given us a miracle.''

I said, ''Oral, stop the car.''

''What's wrong?''

''Just stop the car.''

He did. "Now what?"

"Well, Oral, this is the beginning of something. I feel it, I know it. Let's have a prayer and dedicate this car to the Lord."

Well, we had a prayer of thanksgiving to a God who loved us so much He wanted us to have a good car.

I feel that was really the beginning of Oral Roberts University. Why? Because if we hadn't discovered III John 2, and the Lord hadn't honored Oral's faith for that car, we might still be thinking that Christians should be poor. We might have put up old army barracks on the ORU campus — but who would have wanted to attend? I said that to Oral once and he said, "And I would have died." He's always wanted to go first class — and anyone who looks at Oral Roberts University can tell he does what he believes.

That Scripture was also the beginning of Oral's Seed-Faith concept. Why? If we hadn't learned that God is a giving God, we would never have learned to expect good things from Him. Before you can expect miracles you must believe God is a good God who wants you to prosper. How many needs of others do you think might *not* have been met if the Lord hadn't shown us that Scripture and met our need? We learned that God gives us back everything we give to Him, and more. Why? Because He multiplies the seed sown.

That III John 2 passage is a lesson about God. Read that Scripture again and see how it can apply to your life:

Beloved, I wish above all things that you may prosper and be in health, even as your soul prospers.

We just need to see God in the light of His goodness, and His great love for us . . . then start believing and giving . . . and He will help us prosper beyond anything we can imagine.

Learning to Live by Seed-Faith

Oral and I have always believed Christians should be "giving people" who are willing to go a second mile to help others. To me, there is nothing quite as irritating as a stingy, self-centered person. Throughout our years of ministry — in pastoring, evangelizing, and educating — we have emphasized giving. We believe God honors a giving spirit. The gift is secondary; the act of giving and the spirit of giving come first.

When we started the crusade ministry, Oral would hand out pledge envelopes to people. He felt the Lord would bless them for giving and that the pledge envelopes were a means of getting people into the habit of giving. These pledge envelopes evolved into what Oral called, "My Blessing Pact Covenant with God."

The first time he presented the Blessing Pact was in the Baltimore crusade in 1954. I remember he asked the people to come up and pledge, and told them that if they did not get their money multiplied he would personally return their original pledge. He started with pledges of just $10 and many people came up to give.

Oral told Dr. Myron Sackett about the Blessing Pact the day before he introduced the concept at the crusade. Dr. Sackett said, "Brother Roberts, I want to be the very first one that gives on this Blessing Pact Covenant with God."

"All right, Dr. Sackett. What do you want to do?"

"I want to give one hundred dollars."

"Are you sure you want to give that much?"

"Yes, I want to give that much."

Dr. Sackett gave $100, and Oral told him, "If the Lord doesn't give it back to you, I'll return it."

During the crusade, a man walked up to Dr. Sackett and gave him $300 for his Hebrew Bibles Campaign. Well, Dr. Sackett turned around and gave that money because he felt it was a return from his $100. And, before the crusade was over, another man gave Dr. Sackett $1,000 for his campaign. With that money he bought Hebrew Bibles to send to Israel.

He said to Oral several weeks later, "I wish I had given the one thousand dollars because I probably would have received ten thousand dollars back for the Bibles! I often wonder what the Lord would have done with the one thousand dollars if I'd given it."

For years in every crusade, Oral asked people to pledge $10 to help with the expenses of the meeting, and he always told them to expect a return from God and that if they didn't receive it, he would pay it back. Out of all those years, only two or three persons ever asked for their money back and we sent it to them. The Blessing Pact Covenant became so successful in people's lives that Oral felt he no longer personally had to guarantee each pledge. It has really worked.

During the last ten years, all of the great concepts of our ministry seem to have meshed into one theme. The Blessing Pact was one of those concepts. That God is a good God who wants us to prosper was another. Expecting miracles from God; believing in wholeness in mind, spirit, and body; giving as unto God — all of these positive beliefs have come together in Oral's mind. And God has given him a simple, easy-to-grasp way of presenting his ideas to people. We call the concept Seed-Faith.

Oral wrote a book in 1970 called *Miracle of Seed-Faith* and that one book has found its way into nearly two million homes across this country. God has used it to open hearts and minds to more of God's love, and we praise Him for that!

Just recently, a lady told me how her son had accepted the Lord through *Miracle of Seed-Faith*. She said her son had been very cynical. He was raised in a Christian home, but after his father died, he had become bitter. He quit going to church, and when she turned on our television programs he'd leave the room. He was so unpleasant, he made everybody around him miserable.

"Finally," she said, "I just laid a book down by his bedside. It was *Miracle of*

Seed-Faith. He picked it up and said, 'Whose book is this?' "

"Well, it's Oral Roberts's, but you won't be interested in it."

"I don't know. I might."

The next morning, he came out of his bedroom and said, "Mother, I haven't been to sleep, I read this book all night. It's the greatest book I've ever read. It's changed my whole outlook on life."

That mother was so joyful when she told me this, I couldn't help rejoicing with her. This has happened again and again. People have been blessed by this book.

What is the miracle of Seed-Faith? It's not only an *idea,* it's the practical, scriptural way to live. One of God's greatest laws for nature is the law of sowing and reaping. Farmers have known this for thousands of years. Good seed in good soil yields a good harvest. But farmers also know they can't *make* a seed grow. They can control as many of the conditions as possible, but only God can *make* a seed sprout. This principle is universal and it's a beautiful illustration of the way God deals in our lives.

There are three steps to Seed-Faith which we call "keys." *First, we must realize that God is the One who supplies our needs.* People are only the instruments. God has and uses many instruments, but in the end everything we have comes from God. Whether it's healing for our bodies or healing for our spirits or healing for our finances, God has to supply it. God may use a doctor or medicine as an instrument to bring healing to us. He may use a person as an instrument to pray for us, but neither the doctor nor the person who prays is the one who *heals* us.

We may have a great financial need and a better job may help meet that need, someone may give us something or someone may repay a debt — but in the final analysis, it's God who causes these things to happen. God knows us. He knows everything about us, and He knows the laws of human nature and the laws of the physical world because He *made* those laws. God can make things happen for our good if we openly recognize that He alone is the Supreme Source of our lives.

When we first moved to Tulsa, Ronnie

was four years old. A terrible murder was committed just a few blocks south of the house where we lived and, of course, it was the talk of the entire neighborhood. Ronnie and Rebecca shared the same bedroom and because it was summer I had the window open by Ronnie's bed. Oral was away having a crusade.

One night after putting the children to bed, Ronnie called to me and said, "Mother, I'm afraid that man will come right through this window and murder me."

I said, "Oh, no, Ronnie. Jesus is watching over you. He won't let anything happen to you."

"Now, Mother, you know Jesus is too busy to stand here by my bed all night and watch over me."

"He doesn't need to, Ronnie. He has assigned an angel to you. Your own personal angel stands by your bed all night so you won't need to be afraid."

I remember so well his reply: "Oh, well, if that's the way it is, then I'll just go to sleep."

What a beautiful illustration that was to

me about trusting in God as the Source of all our supply.

The Scripture comes to me, that nothing can separate us from the love of God; neither life nor death, nor things present nor things to come (Romans 8:38). He is our Source and we need to acknowledge Him as such.

The second key is *give so that it may be given unto you.* This principle is embodied in Jesus. Jesus is our perfect example of giving.

All of life is giving and receiving. We stress giving more than we stress receiving, but we have to be able to do both. Some people have been taught to give but never to receive. And some people have received all their lives, but have never been taught to give. The principles of giving work in different ways with different people, but there needs to be a balance.

I believe the Lord wants us to have giving hearts, to give of ourselves and of everything we have in order for us to be free in our spirits, free with other people as He is free with us. We should have giving spirits whether we have $1,000 or $1 — it makes no difference. God looks at the attitude of the heart.

We can give of our time, our talent, our love and understanding, or our compassion. Sometimes giving just a squeeze of a hand means a great deal to a person. That's giving that comes out of our heart. And the Lord told us that if we give and get into the spirit of giving, our gifts will be returned to us.

One day I received a two-pound package of cheese in the mail. When I opened it, I saw it was government commodity cheese from a woman on welfare. I said, "Oral, we can't keep this. This is from a very poor family. Why should she send this to us?"

Then I read the note that was with it. The note said: "Dear Mrs. Roberts: You will probably be wondering why I am sending you this cheese, as my family is on welfare. I know you will be tempted to return it. Please don't because I *have a need to give!*"

That two pounds of cheese suddenly became precious to me. It was a needy mother's Seed-Faith to God. She planted it to get her needs met. Ron Potts, Roberta's husband, walked in and saw the cheese. When I told him the story he said, "Boy, somebody is going to get a tremendous return."

The second key of Seed-Faith also says: *Give as a seed you sow.* What is a seed? One man called it a "condensed, well-packaged plant." I think we need to look on everything we do, every gift we give, as a seed for either a good plant or a bad plant. Like produces like, and the bad things we do come multiplied back to us the same way the good things we do are multiplied back to us.

In the beginning, when God gave Adam and Eve a beautiful garden home, there wasn't one thing they needed that God didn't give to them. They were in a paradise. And then Satan came along, as he always comes along, to steal and kill and to destroy. And he talked to Eve and caused her to doubt God. This is the devil's business. He makes us doubt God and doubt God's Word. Have you ever read a promise in the Bible and then said, "But that's not for me. I know God can do that for somebody else, but not for me." That is the devil at work causing you to say that.

Eve doubted God and then she disobeyed God. That little seed of doubt planted by Satan grew into a plant of disobedience — disobedience which was multiplied back to her and Adam in their expulsion from a paradise.

Doubt, too, can be a seed for rumor. I like to hear good things about people and I don't like to hear evil rumors. Neither does Oral. He hates rumors. He has often said, "I don't want my ears to become slop buckets." When we hear evil things, seeds of doubt about others are planted in our minds, and when those seeds sprout they breed evil. I don't know of anybody who's been blessed by a bad rumor!

But let's look on the positive side. If God is our Source and we are planting good seeds as gifts to Him, then our harvest will be a harvest of *good things*. God is a good God and what He gives us is just like Him — good!

We can learn to expect the good harvest He will send. The third key of Seed-Faith says just that: *Expect a miracle!* Receiving seems to be the hardest part for many people. Some people accept gifts from God more easily than others. Some have been taught not to expect anything back from God. That's why so many people have resented giving. Even today, I hear people say, "I don't go to church anymore because all they want is my money. That's all they're interested in."

If pastors of churches would tell their people to give "as unto the Lord" and as a seed of faith, then expect to receive back from Him, not only would their needs be met, but the churches' needs would be met, too. Many times we feel *obligated* to give to the church and with that kind of giving there isn't much joy. Luke 6:38 says: *Give, and it shall be given to you; good measure, pressed down, shaken together, and running over. . . .* I believe it because I've tried it and it works.

Richard was in bed with the flu once when he was just a teen-ager. When Richard has the flu his sides hurt him terribly. Every time he coughed, his sides ached. One night when he was coughing, I went into the bedroom and said, "Richard, we must have faith and believe God

261

will heal you."

"Now, Mother, just how do you believe God is going to take *this* away?"

"Richard, do you believe when you ask me to go get you a glass of water that I will do it?"

"Well, of course."

"Don't you believe Jesus loves you as much as I love you, and more?"

"Yes, I really do."

"All right then, if we ask Him to heal you, don't you believe He will?"

"Well, yes. Now that you've put it that way, I do."

Then we prayed and he went to sleep — didn't cough another time — and the next morning he went to school.

I'll give you another example. I said to Patti one day, "When you're shopping in some of the antique shops, I wish you would look for an old sewing rocker. If you find one that isn't too expensive, I'd like to go look at it. My grandmother used to have one and I've wanted one all my life."

My housekeeper overheard me talking to Patti, but I never told anyone else about my desire for a sewing rocker. A few weeks later, a chair was delivered to my house. It was exactly the kind of rocker I wanted. A name was on the rocker — a name I didn't know. I said, "Who are these people?"

And my housekeeper said, "The delivery people said one of the ORU seminar guests brought it." She looked at me suspiciously and said, "Mrs. Roberts, did you tell anybody besides Patti that you wanted a rocker?"

"Yes, the Lord."

"Well, He certainly sent you a rocker!"

While I was shaking hands with people at the seminar a man and his wife said to me, "Did you get your rocker?"

"Are you the people who gave me that rocker?"

"Yes. I had just finished making it when we received your invitation to the seminar. The Lord spoke to me and told me to bring you that rocker." Then I told him how I had asked the Lord for one. It touched him and I saw tears come to his eyes.

He had come to the seminar because he needed a miracle in his life and I said to him, "Now, *expect* your miracle. When you give with an open heart, the Lord has promised to meet your needs.''

Of course, it is always easier to believe in some great concept as a theory than to put it into practice. And, even though both Oral and I believe in this concept with all our hearts — and we *know* it works — we sometimes forget who our Source is. Something happened not long ago that shows how *easily* we forget.

One day as I came in from grocery shopping, I said to Oral, ''We're just going to have to do without bacon from now on. Do you know that the price has jumped from a dollar eighty-nine for two pounds to two forty-nine since the last time I shopped?''

Oral stopped me right there. ''Evelyn, the same God who supplied the money for the bacon when it was cheap will supply the money now that the price has gone up. *You* just need to remember who your Source is.''

Oral opens our television programs with a phrase, ''Something *good* is going to happen to *you!*''

When I'm looking to God as my Source

264

and am in the rhythm of giving, I *know* without a shadow of a doubt that something good *is* going to happen to me. God has promised, and He keeps His promises.

We Change Churches

Almost overnight, we lost nearly one-half of our partners.

Letters filled with anger, bitterness, and hurt began to pour in by the thousands. People began to question, "Brother Roberts, have you changed? Do you still pray for the sick? Do you still believe in the Holy Spirit?"

We were accused of being Communist, turning liberal, and bargaining away ORU. More than a third of the income that supported the university and the association dried up; Oral had to go to the bank to borrow money twice just to meet the payroll.

What had we done to bring about such turmoil and confusion?

Oral and I had changed churches. We had rejoined the Methodist denomination.

I say "rejoined" because Oral as a young child was raised in a Methodist church and had worshiped with Methodists as a teenager. I had taught in a Methodist Sunday school while teaching in Texas. Many, many of our closest associates and longtime friends were Methodist. But the majority of our partners didn't know these things or how we came to such a major decision. They saw only the announcement, and *any* announcement without knowledge of its background and motivation brings confusion.

Our rejoining the Methodist Church was a decision made over several years, and after much prayer and discussion between Oral and me. It was not something we did lightly or impulsively. We knew we might have to pick up our Bibles, walk out, lock our doors, and begin all over again.

I felt the coming change as early as 1967 — more than two years before we made the move.

During those months, I was invited to visit several Methodist women's "Circle" meetings. Magdalene Messick, the wife of ORU's first academic dean, was Methodist and she invited me to attend her women's group one time when it met in her home. After that, I visited several other groups that invited me. I just loved being with those women. Not only were they warm toward me, but many were very hungry for more of the Lord. I always enjoy being with people who are hungry for more of the Lord because I am, too. I feel as if I fit in.

It seems to me that some people have received blessings from the Lord for so many years that they take them for granted. Their enthusiasm about God's work has died. When I'm in such a group, I feel stifled. I'm afraid to tell about something fresh and new that I feel the Lord is doing in my life because the blank expressions seem to say, "Oh, I've heard all this for fifty years. Why are you telling me that?" But in these groups of Methodist women, I never felt that way. Instead, I felt a glow and a response — such a feeling of hunger and thirst. I thought to myself, "Here is a group of people who want to *know!* They're hungry to know more about Jesus."

Soon, several of the ladies asked me to

join their group.

"But I don't belong to your church," I protested. "How can I join your Circle?"

"Oh, you don't have to belong to the Methodist Church to join our Circle," they said, "Just be a part of us." And so I was. Charlotte DeWeese, the wife of our coevangelist, and I joined at the same time. Each month, we went with Magdalene to Circle, and I shared some precious times with these women for the next two years. They treated me warmly and lovingly. I could hardly believe that they would accept an outsider as they accepted me.

One day I said, "Charlotte, if I could ever talk my husband into it, I would join this church. There's a friendliness and an enthusiasm among those women that I haven't found among others, and I'm thoroughly enjoying being with them."

She said, "Well, did you know I used to be Methodist? My mother and dad were Methodists. But I know Bob would never join, so that's out for me."

I said, "Well, I'll never mention it to Oral, either, because if the thought ever came to him, I would want it to be from

God. I wouldn't want it to be because of me."

I continued to go to Circle meetings and to speak to several groups around town, but I never told Oral how I felt.

Oral came in one day and he said to me, "Evelyn, what would you think if I said to you that I'm going to join the Methodist Church?"

"I would think you'd gone crazy. Why do you say that to me?"

"The Lord has been dealing with me." And that's all he said.

"Well, you'd just better be *sure,* Oral Roberts, that the Lord's dealing with you before you take a step like that."

We didn't discuss it much, but it was strange how things began to happen. We received a letter from a Methodist lady in which she asked: 'Brother Roberts, have you ever considered joining the Methodist Church? We desperately need your ministry." I thought that was a very strange letter coming out of the clear blue sky. Oral didn't say much about it. He just read it and h-m-m-m-med.

We began to hear from ministers and

lay people across the country. They wrote, "Brother Roberts, have you ever considered joining the Methodist Church? We need your ministry in the Methodist Church. People are open and people are hungry." But still I didn't discuss with Oral what I had said to Charlotte.

Then Dr. Finis Crutchfield (now Bishop Crutchfield), who pastored Boston Avenue Methodist Church in Tulsa, called Oral and said, "Oral, I want to talk to you about something. Would you ever consider joining the Methodist Church?"

And Oral said, "Well, Dr. Crutchfield, I don't know. Why do you ask that?"

"I just feel that there is a place for you in the Methodist Church."

"Well, Dr. Crutchfield, I would really have to pray and know that such a move was God's will."

Oral and I discussed it. And I began to think to myself, "But suppose we *did* something like that — what about all the repercussions that would come from partners and friends? What would happen to us?"

Several weeks later, Dr. Crutchfield

called Oral and invited him to have lunch with Bishop Angie Smith. When Oral came home from that luncheon, he said to me, "Evelyn, do you know what this luncheon was all about?"

"No."

"Dr. Crutchfield wanted me to meet with Bishop Smith because Bishop Smith feels very deeply that I should join the Methodist Church."

"What did you say, Oral?"

"First of all I told Bishop Smith what I believe — that I believe in the baptism in the Holy Spirit, that I speak with tongues every day, and that I believe in healing — all the things I've taught through the years. And Bishop Smith said, 'Dr. Roberts, you don't have to tell me a thing you believe.' I said, 'Well, I won't give up anything I believe.'

"And then Bishop Smith said, 'If you did, we wouldn't want you. I'm about to retire as a bishop, and I feel it would be the crowning effort of my ministry if I could take you into the Methodist Church before I retire.' "

Then Oral said, "Well, Bishop, it's an

honor that you've asked me, but I will have to do a lot of praying and soul searching before I can say 'Yes.' "

But I knew as Oral spoke to me that day that he had already done a lot of soul searching. He never mentions a major decision aloud to me or anybody else until he's done a great deal of praying and thinking. He always seems to make crucial decisions alone, although he may mention the subject he's concerned with to get my reaction. I knew the Lord had been working in his heart.

Soon after, Oral showed me a Scripture which the Lord had given him. It was I Corinthians 16:9: *For a great door and effectual is opened unto me, and there are many adversaries.*

The "adversaries" was the part that bothered me! Oral said to me, "Evelyn, I feel God is moving me to rejoin the Methodist Church."

Then he told me about conversations he had had as far back as 1947 (which I didn't know about) with people who encouraged him to share his message with Methodists. He recalled the warm reception he had received from historic denominations while at the Berlin Congress of Evangelism in 1966. He told me how he felt the Methodist denomination had a place for him, how its membership was diverse enough to let him preach freely from Methodist pulpits. He saw how ORU students might be free to enter into historic denominations and bring to them the fullness of the Holy Spirit. But most important, he shared what God was telling him to do — that secret conviction in his heart and mind that this was God's perfect will for us.

Of course, we also began to discuss what might happen as a result of our changing churches. One by one, longstanding friends came to mind. *What will he say? What will she say? What will he think? What will she think?*

I began to count them on my fingers until, night after night, I could not sleep. All night, friends would come to my mind — people we knew and loved — who would say, "Oral Roberts has given up the Holy Spirit. All these years he's preached the Holy Spirit and now he's changed his mind."

To understand this reaction, you would have to understand why we were a part of the Pentecostal Holiness Church in the first place.

The people who had received the outpouring of the Holy Spirit early in this century — such as my father and mother — found they were no longer welcome or satisfied in their previous churches. Although they had reclaimed a valid biblical experience, the baptism in the Holy Spirit and speaking in tongues, this experience somehow separated them from others in their denominations.

They began to group themselves and a number of "Pentecostal denominations" were founded. Among them was the Pentecostal Holiness Church. The major badge of identification for these groups was their belief in speaking in tongues and the other gifts of the Holy Spirit described in I Corinthians 12 (including healing, words of wisdom and knowledge, faith, discernment of spirits, working of miracles, interpretation of tongues, and prophecy).

Both of our parents had joined Pentecostal denominations after they received the baptism in the Holy Spirit, and Oral and I came naturally into them.

During the crusade days, Oral's ministry was well received by the people in the Pentecostal denominations — but they weren't the only people who attended the meetings. In one crusade we took a poll, and 122 different denominations were represented! As the years passed, we found that more and more of the people were from historic churches — people who were coming into a fuller awareness of the Holy Spirit and His mighty gifts. These "new" Pentecostals saw no reason to leave their churches — something which many people in the established Pentecostal denominations had difficulty in understanding.

Many of these new Pentecostals were Methodists.

Oral certainly didn't change his messages any. We've always held strongly to our belief concerning the Holy Spirit. But somehow the audiences who came to hear Oral's messages changed character as the Holy Spirit began to move in new ways in established churches.

About 1960 we both came into a new

and refreshing understanding of the Holy Spirit. The Lord showed us that a person can use his "prayer language" every day of his life.

While we were growing up, we were taught that a person spoke in tongues at the moment he received the baptism in the Holy Spirit — and he might or might not ever speak in a prayer language again. And suddenly, we discovered that this need not be true. Oral began to share his experience and ideas with others. Oral Roberts University was founded in the spirit of this new understanding, that the prayer language opens up our inner self to God so we can realize all His mighty works for us.

So there we were — experiencing new blessings, sharing them with new and growing audiences, understanding more about the Holy Spirit, and moving into an old-line denomination that did not, as a rule, represent the freedom we personally felt in the Holy Spirit. I just knew our *friends* wouldn't understand, much less our "adversaries!"

But, you know, I was forgetting an

important fact. Evelyn Roberts didn't *have* to make them understand. If the Spirit of God was leading us to take this step, then the Spirit of God would bring the understanding. I had to depend on Him.

I think it is natural to be troubled when we make new moves. When God tells us to do something and it requires a big change, we become fearful. It's difficult to say, "All right, Lord, I'm going to do what You have asked. I'll forget the past and forget other people. I'll just do it." The mind gets in the way.

One night I went to bed thinking about all of the negative things people were going to say. I *knew* they would say them. Oh, I knew it. And I thought, "Well, this is one bout of controversy we can avoid if we just don't make the move."

That night I dreamed I was in a car by myself going down a road through a little country town. There were houses on both sides and some children were in the yards playing. All of a sudden, I became paralyzed. My body became stiff. I couldn't move my arms, my legs, my feet.

When my body stiffened, my foot pressed

the accelerator, and my hand knocked the gear-shift control into reverse, and I began going backward. In the rearview mirror I saw the children. And I kept saying, "Oh, dear Lord, you've got to take over this car because I'm paralyzed. I can't move. I'm going backward. I'm going to hurt somebody. I might *kill* somebody! Lord, please heal me. Stop the car. Do something! I can't move!"

The Lord kept saying, *My hands are on the wheel, I don't need your hands. Just let Me take over the car and everything will be all right. Don't think you have to do it. Trust in Me.* I can take you backward as easily as I can take you forward.

Suddenly my body relaxed. The car stopped. I looked around and nobody was hurt. The children were still playing. The dream was over and I awoke.

The Lord used this dream to say to me, *All right, Evelyn, people are going to say that you're going backward instead of forward* [which is *exactly* what they said]. *But I can take care of your life. Trust in Me.*

I told Oral about my dream. "Oral," I

said, "you know what our friends are going to say, but I'm with you all the way. If you really feel that God wants you to rejoin the Methodist Church, I'm with you."

Then I told him what I had told Charlotte two years before. "The reason I didn't tell you before is that I didn't want to influence you in any way. If you made that decision, I wanted it to be by God's leading. And now I have the perfect consolation that you didn't listen to *me* — but that you listened to the Lord. And that's the way it should be."

We agreed that we would make the move with as little publicity as possible. As far as we were concerned, it was a private decision — one man and his wife changing churches, not a joining of movements. Oral told Mama Roberts and she backed him enthusiastically. (Papa Roberts had passed away the year before.) We also told Bob and Charlotte DeWeese and they backed us 100 percent.

But soon the word leaked out. The rumors began to fly among our associates. We were bombarded with questions and all manner of pleas that we change our minds. As it turned out, we had to speed up our joining the church a couple of months just to end all the excitement.

We joined Tulsa's Boston Avenue Methodist Church on April 7, 1968. When Dr. Crutchfield received us into the church, he said to the congregation, "Now I want to make this very clear. Dr. Oral Roberts is not joining the Methodist Church because he has changed his ministry. He is the same man with the same love for God and people. He belongs to all people because of his compassion and faith. We in this church fully understand this. I have prayed for this day to happen and I could not be happier." We hadn't asked Dr. Crutchfield to say that, but it was exactly the way we felt, too.

The next month, Oral's ordination was unanimously accepted as an elder in the Methodist Church by the Oklahoma Annual Conference.

After we joined the Methodist Church and the letters began to come in from around the world, we had the knowledge and peace that we were doing *God*'s will.

We were very sure that God had directed our move. We would have been desolate without that comfort.

I'm not denying that negative letters and loss of partners hurt us. They *did,* deeply. I'll never forget a meeting we attended shortly after we made the move. We were on a trip overseas and we stopped to attend an interdenominational Christian meeting which many of our former partners were attending. And, oh, the people were so cold. One of the leaders asked Oral to say a few words.

When Oral rose to speak, I felt a chill go over the entire group. Oral felt it, too, and he could hardly speak. He said a few words and sat down.

Then our friend, Clara Grace, rose to preach and her subject was "A Straw in the Wind." At one point she said, "You might call Oral Roberts just a straw out there someplace in the wind, but you had better let him alone. If he isn't doing right, the wind will blow him away. But if he is doing right, time will reveal what God has called him to do."

The next morning at the airport, she told

us, "I feel that God is in what you've done, and I agree with you one hundred percent. Your spirit bears witness with my spirit." The feeling she left with us was beautiful and it helped revive our sagging spirits.

In the months that followed, Oral preached in numerous Methodist churches and at conference meetings. We were invited to England by Methodists there and Oral conducted a week-long conference.

In the years since we became Methodists we have ministered to many laymen's conventions, minister's conferences and conventions. The warmth and openness with which they have received us is just tremendous. We have indeed found an open door.

Today as I write, hundreds of invitations are in Oral's hands from Methodist conferences, churches, groups — their one common request is, "Come to us, Brother Oral, and preach on the Holy Spirit and God's healing power." He's doing it as fast as he can without neglecting the other important phases of our worldwide ministry.

The controversy and turmoil of this move led Oral back to the Bible. He immersed himself in the Gospels and the Book of Acts and the Lord again gave him a new message for the people — the three spiritual laws of Seed-Faith. As he shared this message with Methodists in many cities, his ministry took on a new vitality and commitment. New partners began to warmly receive Oral and his messages. Not only have we been blessed with many new partners, but many of those who left us have returned.

The Lord was not only right about the adversaries, He was right about the "great and effectual door." We have crossed its threshold and find ourselves expecting bigger miracles through Seed-Faith living *every day*. And once again I learned that you can never go wrong if you follow God's leading. He will not lead you into failure.

My Husband Oral

People are always asking me what Oral Roberts is *really* like. I'm never sure if they *really* want to know.

Some people ask, wanting to hear the good things. Some people are after the bad.

One lady wrote to me after she read an article in which I mentioned that Oral let his children ride piggyback. She said, "Mrs. Roberts, we don't want to hear anything that makes Brother Roberts seem like an ordinary man. We have him on a pedestal and we don't appreciate your bringing him down to the level of other men." What could I say? He *did* let the children ride piggyback on our living room floor!

For several years, Oral has been named one of the "most admired men" in America.

But to me he has always been *the* most admired man, so anything I say about him may sound like high praise. I love this man. But one of the main reasons I love him is because he's a real live, down-to-earth human being — and he has his bad moments as well as his good.

Take, for example, Sunday mornings.

Does anything ever go wrong in your house on Sunday mornings? That's when something always seemed to go wrong at our house.

While I tried to get the children up and dressed, breakfast over, and get us all to Sunday school on time, one of the six of us was always in a bad mood or someone couldn't find the right shirt or right belt.

I finally realized it was the devil at work trying to keep us away from church. He really worked overtime at our house.

One recent Sunday morning, I slipped out of bed and turned on the TV to watch our program as usual. It woke up Oral and soon, half awake, he joined me. His first words were, "My clock is twenty-two minutes slow." I remembered having moved some furniture, disconnecting the electric clock, and I admitted that I had forgotten to reset his clock.

The morning had started out on a bad note. In a few minutes he said, "I hear a radio in the background."

"Yes, it's in the bathroom. You can turn it off if it's bothering you."

"It's your clock radio and I don't know how to turn it off." Which meant he didn't want to move. So I got up and turned off the radio.

The thought ran through my mind: I must change the mood of this day. I went to the kitchen and began fixing breakfast. When Oral came in, I could tell his mood hadn't changed.

"Evelyn, this coffee isn't hot."

"Well, I'll pour it out and get you some more."

"No, the pot just doesn't keep the coffee hot."

"I'll admit, Oral, that something has happened to this pot. It doesn't work as it used to."

"Well, you have all week to do something about it."

"Oral, it's difficult to find one that will

keep coffee hot enough for you."

"This is not the only kind of coffeepot made. Try a different kind."

I poured fresh, steaming coffee into his cup and said, "Honey, now you can't tell me this coffee isn't hot. Look at that steam." He grinned and drank his coffee.

Now was my time! I said, "Oral, everything has been wrong this morning because you slept twenty-two minutes longer than you intended. Now that doesn't need to ruin your entire day unless you want it to. You can *will* a change in your mood and in your attitude."

I think for the first time he was able to see what he was allowing to happen. Those words changed his attitude. For the rest of the day he was joyful and not crabby.

All of us are like that at times. Someone has to jolt us out of our bad moods.

My husband has always had a positive attitude. But overall, it's more positive now than ever before. He gets negative only if he's sick. Oral hates sickness and what it does to people. And of course, this is one of the devil's favorite times to inject negative thoughts. When Oral gets a bit negative, it shocks me, and I say to him before I know it, "Oral, you're not like yourself. I can't believe that *you,* of all people, can be this negative." That somehow jerks him to attention.

He'll say, "Oh, am I being negative? Well, I don't want to be. I won't be! I want to be a part of the answer, not a part of the problem." And he snaps out of it.

Too often I think we *sympathize* with people instead of pointing to a solution. When Oral's sick and feeling negative, I could say, "Oh, Honey, I'm so sorry. You've given your whole life to help other people and now you're going to deteriorate before your time." But what good would *that* do? It wouldn't make him feel better. It wouldn't make him think the way the Lord wants him to think. We have to help each other stay on a positive thought line.

A positive attitude has a lot to do with success and enjoying one's surroundings. If we enjoy what we're doing, it has a lot to do with our physical well-being. When we're physically well, we are more likely to have a positive attitude. It's a cycle.

The spirit a person has is very important.

When Oral comes home, I can feel his presence the moment he walks in, even if I don't hear him. His spirit is there. I've heard people say at the office, "The moment he walks in we can feel his spirit." They know he's in the building. The students know when he's on campus. They often tell him they know; whether they actually see him physically that day or not. And this is true of so many people.

In one of Oral's letters from Victoria Falls, he wrote: "David Livingstone was the first white man to see the falls 102 years ago. A statue of him is at the falls and today as I stood looking at the statue, I felt a little as I did at the Sea of Galilee — it's quiet, peaceful. I stood in awe. Livingstone's spirit is really here."

Oral strongly believes that people should work to *prevent* problems just as hard as, if not harder than, to *cure* them. A doctor recently made the statement that "people accept illness as if it were predestined, submitting to it without thought of prevention." This is the way we are about all of life. We seem to accept problems that come along rather than try to prevent them.

Bob DeWeese used to say, "When a cold comes knocking, people go to the door and say, 'Come on in. I have the bed turned back with a hot water bottle in it. I've been expecting you. Come on in and stay with me for a week or two.' We don't do much to prevent colds. We just accept them, and whatever else comes to our door, we open up and invite it in."

Oral likes to deal with a situation *before* it can develop into a problem. At Oral Roberts University, we have found it is much easier to prevent a problem than to cure one.

Oral is not bound by tradition. Now his principles have never changed, but he changes methods quite often. He's always said that the only difference between a rut and a grave is that a rut has the ends knocked out. And he has no desire to stay in a rut. If he finds that a method doesn't work the same as it did ten years ago, he changes. I don't always agree with his methods, although they usually work. I am 100 percent for him in principle.

Everything he does is in the language of the "Now." I think that having students at ORU and dealing with young minds has kept him "thinking young." It has helped both of us. Oral is a well-read person. He reads everything that comes on the newsstands that's fit to read. He keeps abreast of the time. He has a great knowledge of what's going on in the world. He tries to keep his ideas young so that his language will speak to the people as they are living now, not as they would have lived 2,000 years ago.

Oral feels that if the Lord was walking on the Earth right now, He would talk in the language people use now.

He wants everything to be excellent. He likes doing things nobody else has done. When he bought the first tent he said, "I want to get a tent built stronger than one has ever been built before."

He's kept his physical appearance up with the now, too. He exercises regularly and is in good physical shape.

A reporter once said, "No finer specimen is likely to ever grace the rostrum at a convention than the towering six-footer with the raven-black hair and the deep and powerful voice."

I'm not surprised. The raven-black hair

and the towering six-footer part is what attracted me to him in the first place!

During the years of the crusades, Oral ate alone when I wasn't with him because he wanted to keep his thoughts sorted out and conversation distracted him. On one such occasion he went into a coffee shop to eat and a man kept glancing his way. Finally, he got up and came over to Oral's table and said, "If I didn't know better, I would say you are Oral Roberts." Oral just smiled but didn't say a word because he didn't want to lose his line of thought. When the man finished eating, he went to the counter to pay his bill and just as he was leaving, he came by Oral's table and said, "Well, mister, it's better to be thought of as someone great than as nobody at all." Oral never did tell him who he was.

I believe Oral would rather talk to the Lord and pray for sick people than anything else.

He has prayed for me many, many times. It's so natural for him to pray that I never think very much about it. I've had terrific backaches and he has prayed for me and the Lord has healed me.

One time, a knot about the diameter of my thumbnail appeared on the back of my hand. The knot kept growing. I told Oral that I was going to have the doctor cut it out. And he just put his hand over it and said a prayer and then said, "You don't ever have to worry about that any more; the Lord is going to take care of it."

I forgot about it. Then four or five days later, I glanced down and all that was left of that knot was a little sunken place to show where it had been. I still have that place to show what God did.

When the children were ill, we always had prayer in our home. Of course, I took the children to the doctor regularly when they were growing up. We had a family doctor, but when sickness came we had prayer *first*. I always felt the Lord was nearer than any doctor. Many times, the Lord would take care of a situation and we wouldn't have to go to the doctor. Other times, we did go to the doctor. It didn't make any difference to me how they received help — through a doctor or through prayer. The Lord did the healing either way.

Once, when Richard was small, he had twenty-seven warts on his feet and hands. One day I said to him, "Richard, I'm going to take you to the doctor before school starts and get those warts burned off."

Oral was reading a paper and he looked up at me and said, "You leave those warts alone, the Lord will heal them."

A week or two went by and nothing happened, so one day I said again, "Oral, you and Richard better get busy with the Lord on those warts. It's two weeks until school opens and I'm going to take him to the doctor."

Oral said, "Richard, come into the bedroom with me."

They went in and prayed, asking the Lord to remove the warts. A few days later, I thought again about the warts. I said, "Richard, come here and let me check the warts." There wasn't a wart; they were all gone.

Oral is a conscientious preacher. He studies for each sermon as if it were the last sermon he ever expected to preach. Then he asks God for His power to anoint him.

That is why I enjoy his sermons so much. He may use the same subject, but it never comes out the same.

It has always upset Oral to have any disturbance while he is preaching. He believes a sermon should be delivered without interruption. I remember at one of the crusades, the crowd was so large they added some extra seats on the platform behind the preachers and that's where I sat, along with others who couldn't find seats.

Just as Oral began his sermon I heard a woman behind me moaning, "Lord, help him. Lord, help him." I knew in a minute Oral was going to hear her and I didn't know what to do, so I did nothing. I could see Oral with his sharp eyes trying to detect where the sound was coming from. Finally he spotted it and turned around and without missing a word of his sermon, looked at her and said, "Woman, be quiet." Then he turned back around and went on with the sermon as if nothing had happened. I didn't hear any more out of the woman after that.

He is so conscientious about preaching because he says he has no faith apart from

God's Holy Word.

"The only way I can get people delivered is to build up their faith by preaching the Word," he says.

I know his own faith reaches its strongest point just after he has finished preaching. He does his most fruitful praying for the sick following a sermon. He feels he must bring faith to a climax through preaching so that his prayers for the sick will be answered.

I've often been asked how the Lord speaks to Oral. I admit I've asked him about that, too. He answers, "I don't know how to describe God's voice to you, but I know it was God speaking."

He says that God's directions to him are given in military terms, and I believe it, because God knows that's the way Oral is made. God gives directions in a terse, concise way and Oral understands that kind of language. The Lord deals with me in a way completely different from the way He deals with Oral. I could never take orders in military terms and the Lord knows this, so he deals with me in a more gentle way. Each of us is unique. We're all different and that's a beautiful attribute of the Lord. He knows how I'm made because He made me. Nobody but Jesus knows how I tick inside.

I'm glad Oral doesn't know. He has often said to me, "Honey, I would love to know what makes you tick. I'll never understand you as long as I live."

To which I reply, "That's what makes life interesting. You don't know me inside and I don't know you."

Oral often tells an audience, "I am a one-woman man and my wife is a one-man woman."

No truer words were ever spoken. He is the only man I have ever loved.

He has never allowed himself to be put in a position where people could gossip about him. He doesn't smoke or drink and never has. He never went to a parishioner's home when the husband was away at work unless I was with him. If he had to take women of the church home after a service, he always had them ride in the back seat, no matter how old they might be. I remember when he was twenty-three and we were pastoring the church at Shawnee,

298

Oklahoma. Some mornings there was a ten o'clock prayer meeting and several widows much older than Oral attended. Often they had no ride home, so Oral took them home but he made them all sit in the back seat of the car. They had a lot of fun saying, "Brother Roberts is afraid of us. He puts us in the back seat."

He has never said anything uncomplimentary about me publicly — *never*. He's not an *angel,* but he's always uplifted me in other people's eyes. I try to do the same. A good way to break up a marriage is to belittle each other in public.

Oral Roberts believes in being *on time!* On Sundays during the years we pastored churches, he would say, "Evelyn, it's time. Are you ready?" And he'd go sit in the car and honk the horn until I *was* ready, the children were dressed, and we were on our way. We were always the first ones in church. I would be at the piano and Oral would be at the front door greeting people when they arrived for Sunday school. Our children sat in the front row.

Oral never does anything like washing dishes around the house. He's all thumbs.

When he was in Poland, he had to do his own laundry and he wrote: "I have just put out my washing and feel right proud." That was unusual — to say the least.

He thoroughly enjoys sports. On Mondays off, during the crusade days, he usually went fishing, golfing, or horseback riding with our crusade team. He seemed to throw off all responsibility then and relax — laughing and playing pranks.

The ORU Titans (basketball team) have no more devoted fan than Oral. When the Titans win, he feels it's a victory for God, not just for basketball. One reason we have athletics at Oral Roberts University is because Oral feels many men will become more interested in his ministry through the Titans' victories. But he also likes the action of the game.

One young boy asked his dad, a Titans sportscaster, "Do you suppose Mr. Roberts could do anything to make me six feet, six inches tall? Someday I want to be a Titan."

When the ORU Titans defeated Memphis State in Madison Square Garden, the headlines read "Memphis Flunks Oral Exam." Many jokes are made about Oral, but they never seem to bother him. For years there have been sports jokes — claims that "it doesn't rain when Oral Roberts plays golf" and the like. A reporter asked Oral one day which joke was his favorite and he said, "I like them all."

He has a good sense of humor and he doesn't mind laughing at himself. Once, when he was out of town, he stopped by one of those coin-operated photograph booths and took a picture of the front of his head, the back of his head, and then both sides. He put them in an envelope and sent them to me. That's all. He didn't write a word. I laughed for days.

When Oral was away, he always wrote or sent something, maybe just a few words, but always something. From Moscow, his letter read, "Love from me in Moscow. Oral."

He never writes to me when he's in town, though — not even a card for birthdays or Christmas.

One scorching summer day, Ronnie was toddling around our house in his diaper. We were packing boxes and getting ready to sell our furniture and move to North

Carolina. It was a busy day. I had put an ad in the paper about the furniture and people were coming to the door to look at it.

We needed something from town and I said, "Honey, I'll have to go because if people come to look at the furniture, I don't know how much you want for different things. You take care of Ronnie and the furniture and I'll run the errand."

As soon as I left, people came to the door and Ronnie got sick with diarrhea.

A mother would have said, "Excuse me just a moment, my baby is sick," and then would have stopped and cleaned the baby. But Oral was so upset he didn't know what to do. There he was, trying to show the furniture and clean up after Ronnie, all at the same time. When I got home he was very upset. He said, "Evelyn, don't you ever go off again like that and leave me with a sick baby. I can't manage that."

I told him he was learning to be a good father.

One year, Oral was invited to play in the Bob Hope Golf Classic in Palm Springs, California. We both were excited as we packed to go. We had a beautiful place to stay. The weather was between seventy-five and eighty degrees every day (it was seventeen degrees in Tulsa!), and everything was going well. Oral practiced two days and played the first round. The second day of the tournament, one of those Santa Ana winds came whirling in. We'd never seen that much dust. Wham! Oral became ill.

We had an invitation to Bob Hope's home for dinner that evening. Instead, we stayed in our cottage — Oral in bed and I nursing him with hot lemonade and gargles.

He had the second lowest score among amateurs after the first round, but was eliminated from the last two days of the tournament because of that cold.

More than anything else, I felt sorry for myself. It was a brilliant summer day and I wanted so much to be free. Instead, I was cooped up indoors nursing a sick man. "For better or worse" was, at that moment, worse. I know Oral sensed my feelings because he looked up at me and said, "I've ruined everything for you."

Then I felt so guilty. I said, "Honey, without you, I wouldn't have had a chance to be in Palm Springs anyway."

It is at such moments that I realize I wouldn't have been many places without him. Our travels together have led me many places; his positive faith in God has led me farther than I ever could have hoped to go on my own.

When Oral is home, there is at least twice as much work to do, more cooking, more straightening up. Oral's work, his meetings, the office — all are run with utmost efficiency. But his personal things are always scattered all over his room. A hotel maid in Jacksonville came in one day to clean up his room. She took one look and said to him, "Preacher, you just break my heart."

Oral is quick to tell me if something I do displeases him or he feels it is wrong. I do the same for him. Keeping things locked up in the heart doesn't work for us. And when Oral feels the urge to say, "Evelyn, I love you," he says that just as quickly as he points out my faults. We always tell each other what is in our hearts. We have never had secrets from each other.

I'm glad his heart is tender toward the Lord as well as toward me because a small mistake can visibly shake him.

He often says to me, "Evelyn, I know my men feel I'm very hard on them, but the Lord is harder on me. When I make a misstep, I feel him pull me around and put me in my place in no uncertain way."

I remember an incident that happened many years ago. Oral made a mistake in judgment. To me it was a small thing but to him it was big because he felt he had displeased Jesus.

When we retired to our room that night, he said, "Evelyn, I've made a mistake, I've disobeyed the Lord." His face was as white as a sheet.

"Honey, the Lord understands your heart. It wasn't as bad as you think."

"No, Evelyn, I can't afford mistakes. I am God's instrument to help deliver people. My mistakes will hinder God's work. I must make it right."

That night Oral wouldn't eat supper. In our hotel room he sat down on the floor, put his head in his hands and sat there for about a half hour. I wanted to help him, but he felt he had wronged the Lord and only he and the Lord could settle it. He looked up, and I saw that his face was drained of color. His eyes were bloodshot. He looked like a lost soul and my heart ached for him. Suddenly, the tears flowed and he cried so hard that I thought his body would break in two.

From the guilt apparently resting heavily upon his soul, one might think he had committed some terrible sin. Not so. He had merely made an error in judgment, but he felt as if he had displeased the Lord. Jesus of Nazareth is his very life. His first thought is always, "What will Jesus think?"

After he stopped crying, he turned his face toward heaven and began to talk to the Lord. I wouldn't have missed witnessing this for anything. It gave me a glimpse into his soul.

"Jesus," Oral said, "I've made an awful mistake." Then he reached out his hands and it seemed that he took hold of Jesus' hands and said, "Jesus, I've hurt You. I've disappointed You. Will You forgive me, Jesus? Will You tell me everything is all right again?"

He sat there as if in a trance. Then slowly

he turned and looked at me. A great big smile came on his face. He said, "Evelyn, everything is all right. Jesus has forgiven me."

"Oral, I never knew before just how much Jesus means to you," I said.

"Honey," he answered, "if I ever thought I would lose Him, I would rather die right now."

This may seem strange to say, but I've known for many years that Oral has a love for Jesus unlike the love he has for me or the children. But I'm not jealous and neither are the children. His love for Jesus just makes his love for us, his family, more sacred and makes us love him more. The Lord has a magnetic power over him and Oral gives back a love that seems to come from the depths of his soul.

Many people have told me that they have seen Jesus standing beside my husband while he is preaching. Some have seen the Lord's hand on his hand while he prays for the sick. I do not have the slightest doubt of this, for Jesus is the most real person Oral has ever known.

In 1952 Oral wrote an "Open Letter

to America":

America, I have seen the world's hurt. I have felt the heartbeat of lost and suffering humanity. I have heard the voice of God: *"Son, I am going to heal you and you are to take my healing power to your generation."*

I have to go. I have no choice. I am on fire, and I can't stand still. The call of God to deliver mankind rings in my ears day and night. I must go.

I said to one of the great preachers of our day, "What are you going to do with the sick?"

He said, "Oral, I am going to leave them to you."

I said, "Thank you, I'll take them."

I do not know how long Jesus will tarry, nor how long He will let me live. But until He comes, or I leave this world —

Listen to me, America:

I love you;
I have flown your skies,
driven your highways,
walked your hills,
enjoyed your freedoms;

I have preached to your masses,
won your lost,
healed your sick,
given you God's message for
this hour.
Look for me, America:
I will be preaching to you that God is
a Good God and the devil is a bad devil —
that you are facing your greatest
revival and this time it is a revival of signs
and wonders, miraculous healings,
deliverance of soul, mind, and body —
that you will see, and this is a
prophecy, your greatest power is not in
your tanks and bombs, your dollars and
guns, but in your trust and faith in God.
My America:
I am one of your sons
the least of all your sons,
but the spirit of deliverance is
in me,
a consuming fire is in my soul,
a firebrand is in my hand,
faith is in my message.
Look for me, my America:
at the crossroads of your
greatest cities,

in the big tent,
on your radios,
on your television sets,
for God has raised me up to take His
healing power to my generation.

More than twenty years later, that's still
my husband's burning desire — to meet the
needs of people.

Miracles

Expect a Miracle!

How many times have you heard Oral Roberts say that? I've lived with that phrase so long, it has finally sunk in — I *do* expect miracles. Not just occasionally — *every day!*

A long time ago, I thought a miracle was something very special and out of the ordinary. But I've changed my thinking on miracles a great deal, especially since I began studying the Holy Spirit. *God performed many miracles through Jesus, but Jesus didn't call His deeds miracles: He called them "the works of the Father."* Normal, everyday works of the Father. It was the disciples who were awestruck and called his deeds miracles.

I believe that although some things seem big and unusual to us, God looks on them

311

as commonplace. He wants us to have miracles every day. Miracles should become the *norm* for us. Instead of looking for something extra special, we might start considering the *small* miracles that have a big impact on our day-by-day living. A lot of the small things *are* miracles.

When I'm hurrying somewhere to an appointment, I often ask the Lord to save me a parking place. To me that's a miracle. When I slide right into the last parking slot, I give the Lord credit for saving it for me. I know He's concerned about what I'm doing. And I know He is capable of reserving parking spaces.

Several years ago, right after Christmas, Patti and I were to go to the Caribbean where Oral and Richard and the World Action Singers were ministering. Patti had the flu and couldn't leave with the rest of the group. I stayed with her until she could go.

A few days before we were to leave, I looked for my passport and couldn't find it. I knew it had been renewed and returned to me at home, but I couldn't find it any place. I called our housekeeper and asked her if she remembered my putting it someplace. She said, "No, I saw it before Christmas, but I haven't seen it since."

I began looking through everything I could possibly think of. I had stacks of Christmas cards all over the house and I started looking through those Christmas cards, one by one, but I couldn't find it. I looked all that day and the next day. The following day we were to leave and I was about ready to panic. I thought, "Well, I can't go without a passport; I don't know *what* I'm going to do."

I sat down and said, "Lord, *You* know where that passport is. And *You* can guide me right to it. You can show me where it is. I'm going to leave it to *You*. I'm going to commit it to *Your* hands. If I'm not supposed to go to the Caribbean and this is why I'm not finding my passport, all right. I'm willing to stay here. But if *You* want me to go, please help me find that passport."

I didn't think any more about it. I packed and did other things. That afternoon I began thinking about a stack of Christmas cards that I had gone through once, but not carefully. I felt impressed to pick up that stack of cards and go through them again — and I found my passport stuck between two of those cards. Now, to me, that's a miracle.

Some might say it was just a coincidence. I disagree. I don't believe in coincidence. I believe God governs my life and He allows things to happen for a reason. Everything has a purpose. I believe the Lord arranges our lives for us when we let Him. I'm very sure He arranged my life to be Mrs. Oral Roberts. And I give the Lord credit for helping me find that passport, too. He takes care of the big things and the little things — if we let Him.

It all comes to this:

Miracles aren't accidents. They are works of God. Miracles don't just happen haphazardly. They don't fall from the sky into your lap. You don't get a miracle for nothing. Something is required for a miracle, and that something is faith. A miracle comes through faith in God — faith as a seed you plant. God's works are revealed and given to those who seed for them because they love Him.

During our ministry, I've seen many

dramatic miracles of healing, but these miracles happened to people who *believed* God was going to work — or someone else believed by seeding on their behalf.

In 1957 and early 1958 a shortage of funds threatened our ministry. The Abundant Life Office was under construction and suddenly a major loan was not approved. A recession had struck the nation and lending institutions withdrew many of their commitments. We were included in the cutback. A million-dollar loan had been promised to us so we could complete the building, and suddenly there wasn't a cent available.

For the next three months, we faced absolute defeat. The outer walls of the building were up and that was all. We had been paying as we built and when the funds ran out, we didn't know where to turn.

Oral prayed about it and I prayed about it. We released our faith that God could and would work to finish a project that would honor Him. We felt the assurance in our hearts that God would supply. Oral didn't halt the construction even though he was advised to do so. Suddenly, things turned around. Special contributions for the building began pouring in and we received a loan from an unexpected source which let us finish the construction. Once again, God proved to us that *He* was the worker for miracles and that He knew the best methods of bringing about the miracle.

Recently, Oral became ill with the flu. He was miserable. All day he kept saying to me, "Why is my throat *still* sore?"

I said, "Honey, it takes a few days to get over the flu."

"Well, I've been gargling as the doctor said, we've prayed, and I should be well. Why doesn't the medicine work? Why am I still sick? Why, why, why?"

I read the Bible to him. I read some of his own sermons on sickness and healing back to him. I prayed numerous times. I went to the drugstore countless times to pick up aspirin, cough syrup, throat lozenges.

Finally, I told him, "Oral, be patient and stop grumbling. Give the medicine a chance to work and give God a chance to work a healing. Maybe part of your healing will come through rest. Don't

316

be so impatient."

He looked at me and said, "The next time I plan to be sick, it will be without *you* to tell me to be patient!"

I was so amused I had to go into another room and laugh. But then I decided to give him some of his own medicine — so back into his room I went with the Bible and a book he had written called *The Miracle Book.*

"All right, Oral Roberts," I said, "you preach to others about what to do when they're sick. Now you're going to hear your own remedy and what the Bible says."

He cut those blue eyes around at me and said, "Good. I'm listening."

After I finished reading two chapters in *The Miracle Book,* I turned to a portion of Scriputre in James where it says to call for the elders of the church to lay on hands and pray for us when we're ill.

"Oral, we don't have the elders of the church handy, but I'm going to lay hands on you and believe the Lord will raise you up. Do you have faith to believe God will heal you if we pray?"

"Yes," he said, "I know He will."

I got on my knees by his bed and put my hands on his throat and chest, rebuked Satan, and demanded that the sore throat and flu leave him in the name of Jesus. I relied on Jesus' promise, "Ask what you will in My name, *in faith believe,* and you can have it."

I believed, Oral believed. We both knew that God's highest wish was that he be lifted up from that bed. We released our faith in God's ability and desire to work on our behalf. And the flu broke! Oral slept well and by the next morning he was on his way to full recovery. I call that a miracle. It was a normal work of God. It wasn't an accident. It was a direct response to our *believing* that God would work in Oral's body, and we planted a seed of faith by reading and applying the principles of God's Word for a miracle.

Today, we are more dependent upon miracles than ever before. The needs we have are in different areas — the tremendous cost of television and radio production, the monumental responsibility of ORU, and so many other outreaches of this ministry. We *have* to expect a new miracle every day.

And that's the fourth idea I'd like to share with you about miracles: *Miracles* are *for today. Miracles are for* you *today.* I believe that if you learn to call miracles *normal* works of *God,* and believe that God can and will *work* on your behalf, when you can see miracles all around you every day.

Recently, several hundred of our partners here in the Tulsa area gathered for an evening of fellowship with Oral and me and the World Action Singers. The Spirit of the Lord was wonderfully present. After Oral's sermon, he and the Singers laid hands on people and prayed for them. They believed together that God would bless and heal each partner. I sat praying and suddenly realized that I was leaning forward in my seat with the same thrilling interest I felt when we began the crusade ministry in 1947. In one period of about five minutes I saw several miracles of healing, one of them the disappearance of a large goiter.

This thought came to me: Do people realize that miracles are still happening *today?* I've seen miracles for nearly thirty years through our ministry, and each time it's as if it were the first one I ever saw.

As this thought and many others sped through my mind, a new partner of ours, Mamie, rushed up to me and said, "Evelyn, look at this woman. I want you to know that the goiter is *gone.*"

"Of course, it has happened many times before."

"You mean you've seen this happen before?"

"Yes, haven't you?"

"No," she answered. "This is the first miracle I've ever seen in my life."

Then she said, "Just look! Her neck is red; it looks as though it's been on fire. That goiter just melted in front of my eyes."

"Where were you, Mamie, when it happened?"

She answered, "I was standing right next to her in the prayer line. Brother Roberts prayed for her and told her to touch her neck to see if the goiter was gone. When he saw it was gone, he just sent her on as if it were a common-place thing."

I said, "Well, it's because he's seen it happen so many times; he believed God would do it."

Then she turned to the woman who had been healed of the goiter and asked, "How can you be so calm?"

The woman said, "Well, I believed if Brother Roberts prayed for me the goiter would leave."

Mamie took the woman's hand, saying, "I've got to take you back to Brother Roberts. He may not know you're healed."

She took the woman back to the healing line and when Oral introduced her to the crowd, it almost broke up the meeting, everyone became so excited. Then Mamie asked the woman, "Did you come alone?"

She said, "No, my husband and mother are here with me."

Mamie located the family and proceeded to interview them on her own.

"How did you come?" she asked.

"We rode over from Weleetka, Oklahoma, in a truck. The doctor had told me that in a matter of weeks I would choke to death unless I had an operation. In the meantime, we received an invitation to this seminar and I knew if I could get here God would heal me."

Mamie questioned the husband: "How

can you be so calm about all this? Don't you realize your wife has experienced a miracle?''

He smiled, "Oh, yes, I was expecting it to happen.''

Then she asked the mother, "Did you feel the same way?''

"Yes, I did. I knew if we could get my daughter over here God would heal her.''

Several days later, Mamie said to me, "Evelyn, I felt like tearing the place apart because I was so thrilled, but these people just stood there taking it in the calmest way I've ever seen.''

Then she said, "Well, I just started believing God can do *anything* now. Miracles can happen *today*. I started expecting things to happen in *my* life. I've been having trouble with my three teen-agers. Our family communication had seemingly broken down. But Evelyn, since the night I saw that miracle, things have changed. My three teen-agers all have jobs. The youngest has joined a singing group. We're a united family again.''

"Mamie,'' I said, "the reason all this is taking place in your family is that something has happened inside you. This is what a miracle of God can do for a person. You say to yourself, 'If God can remove a goiter from a woman's neck, He can perform a miracle in me and in my home life.' He not only can do the big things today, He can work in all areas of our lives. We need to recognize God at work, ask Him to work, and expect Him to work."

This incident made me realize anew that God's power is not limited. He can do anything. The only limitation is a lack of faith on our part. Of course, it helped to realize, too, that Jesus has not changed. He still performs miracles today just as He did 2,000 years ago. Not only do I see miracles in our ministry, but they are happening throughout the world. It is so exciting to be a part of all God is doing today to reveal himself to His people.

To Oral and to me, too, expecting a miracle has become a way of life. We still see miracles of mighty deliverance. We're also seeing how God can work all the *details* in our lives to His glory.

Remember — miracles are God's *works*.

They aren't accidents. God wants to work for our good in the big things and in the little things. We only need to believe that He can and will work on our lives even now — *today! Expect* your *miracle!*

My Friend, the Holy Spirit

When Oral Roberts University began in 1965, the Holy Spirit was just beginning to fall anew in this country. There was a fresh and sweeping movement among Methodists, Baptists, Lutherans, Catholics, and others in the historic churches.

Oral felt that the Lord had made him a vital link in His great plan to pour out the Holy Spirit in this movement of history. He often said, "Honey, my whole body is tingling with the knowledge that God is going to let people have His great gifts of healing, miracles, discerning of spirits, tongues, prophecy, wisdom — all of them. We are part of the vanguard. Things are really going to start happening."

I could feel everything he was saying. There was such excitement inside me about the Holy Spirit, I could scarcely stand still.

Yet, for many years in the crusades, Oral felt he could not preach about the baptism in the Holy Spirit. Bob DeWeese preached about it in the afternoon services and many people received the infilling of the Holy Spirit at the crusades. But I remember Oral saying to Bob one time, "For the life of me, I cannot preach on the Holy Spirit in the evening meetings. The Lord is leading me to preach *salvation and healing.*"

Which he did.

The Lord's time came, though, when Oral could preach about the Holy Spirit. One night he started toward the pulpit and he told me later the Lord completely took away the message he had prepared. He couldn't remember anything he had planned to preach. The Holy Spirit came into his mind. That night he preached on the baptism in the Holy Spirit. It was the Lord's time to do it.

In every crusade after that, Oral preached about the Holy Spirit in one of the evening services. Hundreds and hundreds of people received the experience we call the baptism in the Holy Spirit, and they took this experience back to their churches. Many of the people belonged to historical Protestant churches, or Catholic churches. We began to hear from people and groups about how their new interest in the Holy Spirit was spreading to others.

Oral certainly doesn't take credit for starting the Charismatic Movement, but I feel he was an important instrument in God's outpouring of the Holy Spirit in the world today.

Since he has preached and taught about the Holy Spirit for so many years, many people come to us asking for more information about the works of the Holy Spirit. Oral teaches a course at ORU entitled "The Holy Spirit in the *now*" and more than 2,000 persons attend this class. This course is ORU's first endowed academic chair. The late Lord Rank, an English film maker and outstanding Methodist layman who received the Holy Spirit under Oral's ministry, was very interested in the work of the Holy Spirit at ORU and established this chair as a lasting personal *and* academic monument to the Holy Spirit. Oral's lectures are now taped for viewing on cable television, and cassettes and books have been distributed around the world in answer to requests from persons who want to know more about the Holy Spirit. Entire denominations in India and other countries use these video cassette tapes to spearhead their desire for the Holy Spirit to work more effectively in their movements.

I often help Oral with the class discussions that follow his lectures, and people in many places have come up to me, hungry to know more about who the Holy Spirit is. This is what I tell them:

The Holy Spirit is the One that brings us to Jesus. He enters us when we accept Jesus as our Lord and Savior. He lives in us.

With Him comes an inner knowledge of a prayer language. But until we release and use that new language, it never does us any good at all. The language is there, but unless we release it, we often feel that our prayers are not heard and we don't always know how to pray (Romans 8:26).

When we release this prayer language — speak it and put it to use — it releases our spirits inside. We call that releasing experience the *baptism* in the Holy Spirit. I don't believe we have to *go* somewhere to seek the experience — we just have to release what's already in us. We call it the *baptism* because at that time, many people feel completely immersed in a feeling of love and compassion.

Some people call this prayer language *speaking in other tongues* because when the people in the New Testament churches received this outpouring of the Holy Spirit on the Day of Pentecost, they referred to their new languages as new or other *tongues.*

One of our ORU students said it this way: "When I received this experience, I spoke in a beautiful, musical language. I felt a bursting of happiness and fulfillment that I'd never before known. I found as the weeks went by that I was able to pray in my new language almost at will. I sometimes leave my studies and walk about the campus and pray in my new language to rest my mind. Then I return refreshed and able to concentrate on my studies. My prayer language is a means of physical and mental rejuvenation and an experience of happiness for me."

A girl told me just recently that she received the baptism in the Holy Spirit while at ORU. She said, "Before that, I could not understand the Bible. I'd pick it up and read it, but I didn't understand what it was talking about. Now, I open it and the meaning is as plain as day."

This is what the prayer language does for me, too, and I think it does that in some form for everybody else. It not only releases my spirit within, it brings about a new understanding in my mind. The Bible is made clear to me and I can understand things that have puzzled me. I have a new sense of inner power that comes with a new understanding.

I remember hearing Hal Hill, a friend of ours who is a scientist, say that he had been at Cape Kennedy during the launching of one of the Apollo flights. The rocket started up and then something went wrong and it began to come back down and crash. Hal had worked on that rocket, and he said, "I knew the Lord and the power of His Holy Spirit. The way that rocket started to fall — I knew it would surely kill everybody standing there watching. So I quietly began speaking in tongues and saying in my mind, 'Lord, You can guide this and take it completely away from where it is headed. I believe You will do this!' Before my eyes, the rocket twisted and fell in a different direction. It didn't hurt any of the spectators.''

For me, an experience has to be practical or it isn't any good. I know from personal experience that when I have a problem I can't solve within my own intellectual power, I can pray in the Spirit and He illumines my mind and I get an answer. Sometimes my *mind* doesn't know the answer and isn't open to an answer from God . . . but if my spirit is open to God, God gives me an answer in that way.

Many times when I speak in my prayer language, I become aware of things that aren't right in my life. I become convinced of things I'm doing wrong — or not doing — and I can confess them to God — and feel the sweet peace of His forgiveness.

I'll never forget a sermon Tommy Tyson, our first chaplain at ORU, preached about prayer and the Holy Spirit. In fact, it was during the first week of the first semester of ORU's first year. He said:

Prayer is the work of the Holy Spirit. If we learn to pray as Christ did, we can do what He did. Prayer is the continuing atmosphere of the lifeline. It is the breath of God in our lives. Dedicated Christians know so little about prayer. Our Christian life begins when we think of our risen Lord more than the person we're praying for. Anyone can pray when the presence of God tips the cup and the glory runs down the sides of the soul, but the Christian should pray always.

One way to pray is the Prayer of Affirmation. We use God's promises in the Scriptures to remind God of His promises. David prayed this kind of prayer, and he said, *"Thy word have I hid in my* heart." He didn't say, "Thy word have I understood in my mind."

Hiding God's Word in my heart, where it can be quickened by the Holy Spirit, is what I want to do. Tommy went on to say,

"We have one basic responsibility. If we're not in union with Jesus, it is our responsibility to get in union and stay in union. Only one thing separates us from God — SIN. The Holy Spirit deals in specifics and He will show us specifically our trouble and our sin."

There is so much to learn about the Holy Spirit! The Bible speaks of the Holy Spirit's fruits as being love, joy, peace, long suffering, gentleness, goodness, faith, meekness, and temperance (Galatians 5:22). I don't know of *anyone* who couldn't use *more* of those attributes!

The Holy Spirit's gifts, too, are exciting: words of knowledge and wisdom, working of miracles, faith, healing, prophecy, tongues and interpretation of tongues, and discernment of spirits (I Corinthians 12).

I can't understand when some Christians say, "I don't want to know more about the Holy Spirit." I don't understand why they want to limit themselves when God has so much for all of us. I never want to stop learning about the Author of miracles, the power of God — the *goodness* of the Holy Spirit.

A Family of Partners

Breakfast is a very precious time in our home. That is when Oral and I read much of our mail and prepare answers to partners' questions and try to write something to help them get their needs met. We often discuss a letter, taking it as a whole to determine the sense of what is being said. We could never answer every detail, but we try to get a feel for the total problem.

We take care of a great deal of the day's business by telephone at the breakfast table. Often, we discuss items in the newspaper and work on publications. Many of our Daily Blessings have been created as a result of something said at breakfast. Oral will give me a new thought and I call the writers who help with our publications and they put it in the form of a Daily Blessing. Thousands of people read Daily Blessing at the breakfast table, and we often feel as if we are gathered around a large table with them.

I love the people who support our ministry. We call them our partners. I feel close to them in a special way. Their letters to us uplift us when we are discouraged — and when they are discouraged, we feel for them and want to do all we can to help them by answering them and letting them know that God cares too.

One woman wrote to us:

Thank you from every part of my being for letting me write to you and open up my heart to you. You bring God so close to each of us. I have never heard anyone with such positive thoughts and attitudes about religion. Fear has often been used to sway beliefs and a lot of religion is really forced on people. But the way you present beliefs instills a desire in me to be a part of God's world.

Another letter read:

Brother Roberts, I was so tremendously moved after reading your last magazine that I thought, "Lord, if Brother Roberts only *knew* how much we love and appreciate his efforts through the years." And the Lord seemed to speak to me and say, *Well, you tell him for all the countless others who really want to tell him and don't.* So — you have been received by kings, presidents and heads of state all over the world, but let me be just a voice out of the great multitude of common folk to say to you, for the Lord and all of us — Thank you.

One lady wrote and said:

Mrs. Roberts, God has met my needs through hearing Brother Roberts preach. My little boy and I were healed in the Augusta Crusade. At one time, I was at the point of committing suicide. It was then I first heard Brother Roberts. His telling me about God's love transformed my way of thinking.

One partner sent me a pair of ceramic doves, and the little note enclosed read, "I made these for you in ceramics. I want you to know how much your witness helped me at the time of my mother's death last year."

During one of the crusades, someone handed a note to Oral, which said: "Brother Roberts, if you have ever been at the end of your rope and then *suddenly* found new hope and new courage, you can understand what this crusade has meant to me. I thank God for your humility before Him and for the work you're doing."

These letters mean a great deal to me. When I get "low" sometimes, these words cheer me up. I sense in these letters that these people love us as much as we love them — and that we aren't working alone. We have partners who are working with us — in prayer and in support of the ministry projects and Oral Roberts University.

Many of our partners join with us for weekend seminars at ORU. As many as 2,000 persons have come to the campus to find out more about Seed-Faith living and the Holy Spirit. I love it when we can share face-to-face. Only those who have supported us and shown a real interest in what we are doing are invited, because while they are here they are offered a Seed-Faith project to sponsor, and we wouldn't want to offer this to people without an interest in our ministry.

The Sunday-morning healing services at the seminars are very special to me. The show of God's power to move a human being is so great. At a recent service, I sat high in the balcony of ORU's Mabee Center and after the service was over, I wrote my impressions of what I had seen:

What a beautiful sight to see such a highly organized procession of people going to the front for the laying on of hands. Oral, Richard, Patti, the World Action Singers, and hundreds of students lined up to help people release their faith and just to love them as they came for healing.

Such miracles! The faith released! The moving of God's spirit! Carlton's inspired singing of "Hallelujah!" [Carlton is an ORU student and World Action Singer.] Our wonderful staff, faculty, students, and retired residents of University Village who volunteer their services to help our guests get into line.

Many of our seminar guests believe God heals in a general way, but they have never seen specific healings such as those in this morning's meeting.

A lady went through the prayer line walking with a crutch. Oral said, "Sister, lift one leg. Now lift the other." She didn't understand; he called her back and said, "Get your faith into action. Move yourself — you may not need the crutch." Her faith was released and she realized her legs were being healed. She gave up the crutch and almost danced with joy.

Many minutes later, I looked across the auditorium to see her swinging her crutch back and forth.

Another lady with a cane came toward me after being touched. Her husband said, "Mrs. Roberts, come see our miracle. My wife has been in a wheelchair five years, but look at her now. She's using a cane and her legs are wobbly, but see how the joy shines on her face! She's on her way."

The anointing of the Holy Spirit is tremendous.

These services carry me back to the early days of the crusade ministry. I know anew: Jesus never changes. He is the same yesterday, today, and tomorrow.

Oral Roberts University — Facing a New Challenge

Oral hadn't even finished high school when we married, but he read every book that fell into his hands. He finished high school and went to college after we had two children. To a great extent, he is a self-educated man.

As long as I've known Oral, he's been interested in schools. During our first years of marriage, he often said he intended to build a school someday. We always looked for the colleges in the cities we visited during our travels. He wanted to see how the campuses were built.

From 1958 to 1960 Oral began seriously to consider building a Bible school for foreign students. His idea was to bring young men and their wives to America for a four-year training period, and then send them back to their own countries as ministers. He envisioned lakeside cabins for them to live in. I was never very enthusiastic about that idea, although I never discouraged Oral about *anything* he felt God might want him to do. Many times I haven't *understood* his projects at first, but with time and prayer, God has helped me to *encourage* him.

Until about 1960 I had never been with him in those intimate times when the Lord spoke to him. But one evening when we were eating dinner during the Norfolk, Virginia, crusade, Oral suddenly seemed totally unaware of my presence. He shoved his chair back, hurried to our room, sat down, and began to write. For the next eight days he wrote the words as the Lord spoke them to him.

Among the things God said to Oral was, "Build Me a university. Build it on My authority and on the Holy Spirit. Raise up your students to hear My voice . . . go where My light is dim . . . My voice is heard small, and where My healing power is not known. You must find a way to enter into all nations, and I say *all* nations, with My Word of healing."

Of course, neither of us could understand all that was involved. But we have learned that when God tells us to do something, we have to obey Him. We don't always know what we are to do, but God leads us step by step.

Oral really had no choice in whether to build ORU. The only choice he had was to say, "All right, Lord. You've told me to do this, but I can't do it and I'm not going to," or to say, "Okay, I'll try." He had dedicated his life to following God and obeying Him, so he had to do what God told him. And God said, "Build Me a university." Oral said to me once, "I feel like a little puppet because I choose to stay in His will. Therefore, the Lord moves me around where He wants me to go."

When he first started sharing with people the plans he had for a university, everybody he talked to said it couldn't be done.

God had told him to build the university on God's authority and on the Holy Spirit. He asked the Lord what He meant by "on the Holy Spirit." The Lord showed him he was to teach about the Holy Spirit and that the university was to have Spirit-filled faculty members and Spirit-filled members on the board of regents. The Holy Spirit was to be the focal point of the entire university.

People adamantly told Oral he would never find enough faculty members filled with the Holy Spirit to staff a university. In those days, Ph.D.'s who admitted to being filled with the Spirit were scarce. Nothing that our well-meaning friends ever said to him daunted his spirit. He believed God would provide the right people. Today ORU has nearly 200 full-time and part-time Spirit-filled faculty members — and over 50 percent of the full-time faculty members have earned doctorates.

Jesus gave Oral the guidelines about rules and regulations for the honor code and the dress code at the University. We both felt these rules were standards that could pull families back together rather than push families apart. Society was in a state of rebellion then. The Hippy movement was in full bloom. Long hair was popular. The establishment was out and families were being pulled apart. ORU was established for students who really care about their families and about the Lord. It was built for students who cared about how they look and about the effects of their actions on others. Oral wants students who look as if they feel good about themselves and who act in a way so as to pull families back together.

And again, people told us, "You'll never get students. You'll never find young people who are interested in going to a school where the rules are that strict."

The first year, we had 300 students. And they didn't fall into any traps. They knew what ORU stood for and they knew the rules. We invited high school students to the campus from across the country to see what ORU was like, and we didn't smooth anything over or entice them to enroll under false impressions.

We told those students, as we tell them today, "This is the way it will be if you come to ORU. There are certain things you *must* do and certain things you must *not* do. You have to choose our life-style to be a student here." And now more than 6,000 students apply to ORU each year. We have 3,000 full-time students who come from every state and over thirty foreign countries. Our residence halls are bursting at the seams. In fact, two new twelve-story dorms are under construction right now to house 750 more students.

When we began plans for the university, people couldn't understand where the money was going to come from and, I have to confess, I didn't either. Oral and I would take long walks over the acreage that is now the campus and he would tell me the hopes and dreams he had for a university dedicated to God in a whole-man concept of life.

I would say to him, "Honey, do you *really* think God will supply the need for every building you want to build?"

His answer was always, "Evelyn, it's not how much it will cost or where the money is coming from, but whether God wants it done and wants us to do it."

"Oral, are you absolutely convinced that God wants you to do it?"

"Evelyn, I'm as convinced as I've ever been about anything in my life."

Money has never been a real concern to

Oral. He has always said, "The Lord has plenty of money. The Lord needs people. If I can get the right people, the Lord will supply the money. He knows where it is."

And it has happened just that way. I won't say that there hasn't been a struggle at times. Every building on campus has had its moments of struggle. There's a struggle before each one begins. Oral prays and prays to know it's the right thing and finally he gets enough faith to dig a hole. No money, but we have a hole in the ground. And then *my* troubles begin. I know what's coming.

In the middle of construction, there comes a letdown. There's been one for each building. The Lord never seems to let us have enough money in the beginning to finish the entire project. He lets us start it and then He lets us come about to the middle of it and He allows a second time of struggle.

At times we've reached the point where we knew we couldn't pay the construction people their next paycheck and we've had to shut down the construction. The devil fights us on every building. He will not give up. He says, "This is one I'm *not* going to let you put up." And Oral walks the floor again, literally, and prays and prays, "Lord, this is Your project. You told me to do this. Help me."

I have questioned Oral many times, "Oral, are you *sure* the Lord told you to build *this* building? Are you sure it's the Lord?"

"Yes, I'm definitely sure it is the Lord."

"Okay, then if it is of the Lord, it's His project. Turn it over to Him and quit worrying about it." Of course, it's easier to tell him not to worry than to quit worrying myself.

But we hold on and eventually the money comes in and the building is finished.

With each new building I think, "Surely this time. . . . We've been through so many struggles, there won't be a struggle this time." But every building is the same.

Our partners have been wonderful. Of course, I know the Lord has nudged them to give or they wouldn't give. But without our Seed-Faith partners all over the world, we never could have built anything.

The buildings for the university began

going up in 1962 and we were ready to open in 1965, with 300 students, five buildings, and a faculty and staff of fifty persons. What a thrilling sight it was to see the students converge on the campus for a week of orientation. I recorded many things in my diary:

Last week was an important, historic week. For years we have looked forward to the opening of Oral Roberts University and at last, the dream has come true.

We began with the Orientation Banquet for the president, faculty, and students on Tuesday, September 7, 1965, at 6 P.M. Many special guests were present — some from the state education office, some of the Regents of Higher Education in Oklahoma, and some representing the news media.

Oral gave the main address. It was a masterpiece. Especially Rebecca and I know how important this speech was to him.

After dinner, we went to the Auditorium for devotions and Holy Communion. It was proper that the academic part be given in the dining room and the spiritual in the Auditorium. The receiving line included all the faculty and their wives. Each one greeted the 300 students marched through.

Wednesday, Thursday, and Friday were used for placement tests and registration.

On Thursday evening, the students had a hootenanny on the lawn. Oral and I went over and sat on the grass with them. They had fun and so did we. We had doughnuts and lots of milk, and after refreshments, Tommy Tyson, the campus chaplain, led us in devotions. We made three circles, one inside the other. The students prayed for us and Oral prayed for them. There was a closeness that everyone felt.

Although the university has grown rapidly, there still is a unity and closeness in the students. They believe in a common reason for being, and that is a great strength. ORU students know what the university stands for and they stand behind the university or they wouldn't be here.

I think the life-style of ORU is great for

our particular age. We are living in a permissive society where children have very few values. They are looking for something to hang on to. They are looking for the discipline that they may not have had at home. And one thing you can say about ORU — students know what they can do and what they can't do. To me, this gives a sense of security.

I think the life-style points to a positive way of looking. It's an "up" attitude and I like that. ORU isn't wishy-washy. The teachers don't say, "Do anything you like, everything goes."

ORU students don't drink, smoke, gamble, use profanity, or use narcotics. They dress neatly for classes and they are expected to attend classes and chapels regularly. They are also required to take physical education courses and exercise their bodies.

We have a new Aerobics Center, recently dedicated in honor of Dr. Kenneth Cooper of Dallas who found the aerobics concept and started an aerobics program for the air force. Aerobics is a plan by which students, faculty, and staff get points for running, jogging, swimming, bicycling, or walking (as in my case).

These students are after a wholeness in life — where the body, mind, and spirit are strong and bound together in harmony. And central to everything is the Lord.

In the center of the campus is a beautiful Prayer Tower where prayer goes up day and night. The students must pass by this tower of faith and strength on their way to and from classes.

I felt very comfortable when Roberta was living in the dorm. I felt very secure knowing that there was a curfew and she had to be in that dorm for the night. I felt certain that she would keep the rules of the university as a student and that those rules would eventually help her life to be directed in the right way. I don't believe there's anything on the ORU campus that will lead a young person in the wrong direction.

I know some people say, "Well, how is a student ever going to be strong as a Christian if he goes to a place where they're taught about the Lord all the time? When is he or she going ever to show maturity?" Well, the students leave campus weekends, literally infiltrating Tulsa and areas 100 to 300 miles away, dealing with life as it is, with people who have all kinds of needs. This gives them toughness. Also in my thinking, there's plenty of time after college to demonstrate maturity. When students graduate from ORU, I feel that they have *a solid foundation* on which to build a life.

Many students come to college without goals or purposes. Find out how many times they change their majors and you'll agree! They're floundering around trying to decide which way to go. The right person can send them in the right direction and the wrong person can send them in the wrong direction. A professor at Stanford told Ronnie and a group of students that they would have to "get off their God kick" and that if they came to his classes with a strong religious background, he would see that when they left, they'd have none.

To me this is wrong! I would never try to change a student's church denomination. I think the denomination he or she belongs to is private business. I would say only this: At ORU, we try to help students have a close relationship with Jesus Christ. They can go to any church they desire or choose any vocation, but we want that relationship with Jesus Christ to be right.

ORU students seem like my own children. They are very precious to me. When they hurt, I hurt.

One of the things I appreciate is that we have students from every race and every denomination and yet we all love each other. There is no race discrimination and we all feel comfortable with each other.

Some of our students have already gone to meet the Lord — some in deep tragedies, some by illness. One such precious girl was Joyce, who sang for several years with the World Action Singers. She was a great blessing to all of us during the six years she sang with the television group. She sang right up to the night before she died.

We get some students at ORU who are holy terrors. They keep the rules — but it's a *real struggle* for them. And many times, we never know how these students turn out. One such boy wrote to us telling us how he met a Buddhist man in Korea who was dying from tuberculosis. He was saved and healed through reading Oral's life story. This former student ended his letter: "Thanks again for the books you sent. You and your husband will never know the lasting influence you have had on my life." This boy is now a minister of the gospel, pastoring a church, and doing evangelistic work.

I love to read the students' letters to us. They bless us, but I think the letters also show how precious these students are. One boy wrote to Oral:

O.R. (Our affectionate name for you.) We love you and are supporting you, because you are searching for the truth in dealing with evil. God will richly bless you. John 16:32 says, "Yet, I will not be alone, for the Father is with me. I have told you all of this so that you will have peace of mind and heart. Here on earth you will have many trials and sorrows, but cheer up, for I have overcome the world." It may seem the walls crumble around you sometimes. But remember, Christ won't crumble; He's our rock. O.R., just put your cares in the Lord. He is completely in control of everything and He hears your cries.

A dear ORU girl wrote this to me:

When I came to ORU as a freshman, I arrived on the evening of the dinner during which we were to meet you and President Roberts. I arrived too late and missed the dinner. I remember walking down the concrete walk which leads to the Prayer Tower. I looked up and saw the eternal flame atop the Prayer Tower, and I could have sworn that I was in heaven. My dad and brother were with me and they went to get my luggage. As I stood waiting for them, I saw a couple coming down the cafeteria stairs.

I didn't want to seem starry-eyed so I ignored them. But they headed right toward me. I turned around and found myself looking straight into the eyes of Oral Roberts himself. You gave me a Mother hug, which I'll never forget. I did get a reception, even though I missed the dinner. You probably don't remember this, but I'll never forget it.

Another student wrote:

In the past few days, God has impressed me with a need to pray for you, and to pray for the university for which I am so thankful. I wanted you to know that you're being lifted up by me in prayer so that your faith might be strengthened, your mind cleared, and your entire being infused with the power of the Holy Spirit.

And these are still other letters from ORU students to me:

Dear Mrs. Roberts — I transferred to ORU after two years in another college. I have been baptized in the Holy Spirit this summer. A whole new dimension in my relationship with Jesus has been opened to me after being a Christian for ten years. Seeing you in the Holy Spirit class and on tape, I have been impressed to write you and tell you how special you are. I relate to you better than your husband. Also, I see in you someone that I would like to be — a warm, down-to-earth woman of God who knows her Lord. I praise the Lord for you, in whom I see His life and power and love.

I want to thank you for coming to our dorm and sharing God's Word of wisdom. You were an answer to prayer for several of us. We love you greatly. Thank you very much for sharing with us at devotions last Wednesday. You answered a lot of questions, brought to mind many more, and really started us thinking about our role today as Christian women.

Your talk made me feel very special as a woman. Thanks so much for giving us such blessed advice. I hope my marriage is as happy as yours. We love you.

Thanks so much, Mrs. Roberts. You

did a lot to inspire and unify our wing. [A wing is a section of the dormitory.] I'm praying that God will grant you the time to complete your book under His inspiration and glory. [Thank *you*. He did!]

Since I, too, was a mother of college students, the letters I have received from ORU parents have been equally precious to me. One mother wrote:

I feel compelled today to write to you out of the gratitude that fills my heart as the mother of two ORU students. I truly believe that one of the reasons that God raised up this university of universities was so my children might be educated there.

I have been feeling the burden you must feel in your responsibility of heading a university such as ORU — a university born in the heart of God with a dynamic potential for literally turning the world upside down. All the forces of the evil one are, and will be, arrayed against your efforts. But as God continues to increase your faith, holds you steadfast, and raises up an army of staunch partners to assist you, you cannot help but accomplish His purpose. I rejoice that I can help share the responsibility of ORU. I know that as God bids, He enables.

Occasionally I go to the Prayer Tower to take a guest to see the Abundant Life Mural and the slide presentation about the university. I'm always amazed at the impact these presentations have on me. Recently, I went and when Richard, who narrates the presentation, said, "The dream at ORU has not died," I couldn't help but say, "Yes, Lord. Don't let that dream *ever* die. Keep it fresh in our minds, with the vision undimmed. We know that where there's no vision, the people will perish. And rather than set our eyes on the magnificent buildings, let us always keep our goal in mind. Let us keep our eyes on Jesus and follow in His footsteps."

One man said to a friend of ours, "I'm not sufficiently informed on his approach to salvation to comment on it. And I'm not ready to join his troops. But he *has* done something with ORU. And as startling as it is, it's only a beginning."

I couldn't agree more. ORU is now twelve years old. Enrollment is increasing each year and new buildings are still going up. I can see the impact that ORU students are already having in their communities and around the world — but I also believe in what ORU graduates are going to do in the years ahead:

They will be taking a positive message of faith in God where God's light is dim . . . His voice is heard small . . . and where His healing power is not known. They will enter all professions . . . going into every man's world . . . and enter into all nations with the healing power of God.

The greater purpose of Oral Roberts University is only *beginning* to come to fruition.

Busy Days

One day while I was shopping, a woman overheard me say something to the cashier and turned around quickly, saying, "That's Evelyn Roberts's voice." For many years, unless I was with Oral, I was not readily recognized until I opened my mouth. If I did, people instantly recognized my radio voice. How I wish that were still true.

Today, with my exposure on television, I am frequently recognized. I am a private person at heart and I have to admit that a life in a goldfish bowl is not appealing to me at all. I'm a normal woman who would prefer to live a quiet, wife-mother-grandmother life. As much as I love people, I often long to be alone and out of the public eye.

Sometimes I wish I could fly a thousand miles away from everything — from the university, from the office, from everybody I know.

When I've talked and prayed and listened to the desperate needs of several different people in one day, I can really become what I call "people weary." I don't *at all* mean that I get tired of *people* — I just get so *weary* in my dealing with people and with a busy schedule that I can't give any more and I must rest. Because I love people and want to help them if I can, I've had to learn to take control of time. I've had to learn to make times for work and times for rest — times for people and times for solitude.

Some days, life seems to go in a circle. *You* know those days. We all have them. As I write this, yesterday was just that kind of day. My housekeeper was sick and didn't come to work. So I had the dishes to do after breakfast, beds to make, the three phone lines began ringing constantly, and all the while I was trying to get ready for the morning chapel service at ORU in which I was to take part.

An associate of Oral's was coming to the house for an appointment and while Oral was on one phone, I was answering doors and the other two lines. As I left the house for chapel, I yelled, "I'll be back as soon as chapel is over to fix your lunch before you have to leave."

I rushed home after chapel and he was still on the phone. The other two lines began ringing the moment I walked in the house. I fixed his lunch hurriedly and we raced to the airport so he could catch his flight. "Now," I thought, "maybe I'll have a free afternoon."

A glass of buttermilk and a sandwich later, the phone rang to remind me I had promised to counsel with a woman who had mental problems. I'd forgotten to put the appointment on my calendar, and had arranged to meet with Patti about ministry business — but I juggled my schedule to see the woman, and met with Patti at five thirty. I desperately wanted to work on this book, but the entire day was one rush after another. University business, ministry concerns . . . Oral seems to have fifteen jobs and I try to help him do them all and at times it is very frustrating. You know what those days are like!

Because of days like that, I have learned I can handle only one day at a time. I cannot think about my schedule for tomorrow or the next day. If I do, I get frightened or nervous or exhausted in advance.

I read a story about an alcoholic. He went to Alcoholics Anonymous, and they said to him, "Can you live without drinking for one day?" And he said, "No, I cannot."

"Can you live without liquor for one hour?"

"No, I can't."

"All right, can you live without it five minutes?"

"Oh, yes, I believe I could live without it for five minutes."

"All right, then begin with five minutes."

So he did without liquor for five minutes, and he said to himself, "I've done without for five minutes. I think I can do without for another five minutes."

The five minutes stretched into an hour. And that's somewhat the way I want to live my Christian life. If I can live a Christian life for a day, that's all the Lord expects of me. Tomorrow will only be a today when I get to it. I don't avoid making long-range plans. We have to have those. But God has not promised tomorrow to me and I must do all I can today and keep my mind on the work at hand.

Oral once said to me that he wanted to live each day of his life as if it were his last day. "That way," he said, "like St. Paul, I will have finished my course (II Timothy 4:7)." I think that's a pretty good way to live.

On those busy, frustrating days, I also realize anew how important it is for me to get off in a room by myself — close the door and close out everybody. Rushing from one thing to another can give me a severe headache if I don't do this. And I need the time to think and study, too, no matter who is in the house. Sometimes I have to say, "I'm sorry. I have to have an hour to myself. I have to study." And people understand. I go into my bedroom and unplug the phones so I can clear my mind and put my priorities straight.

When I get away and close everybody out, I talk to the Lord and read Scripture.

I even have a little worship center in my bathroom. I have a Bible and a verse of Scripture that hangs on the wall there. If I go into my bathroom and lock the door, nobody comes knocking! It's the only quiet place in the entire house sometimes.

When a person is busy in the Lord's work, it's just as easy to get frustrated as it is in any other type of work. You can get to the point where everything seems worthless. You think, "I'm not able to do this job. I'm not doing it right. I want to get away from here." This is when I have to sit down and get quiet before the Lord, put my priorities straight, and see what *is* important.

Now Oral has a power of concentration that I don't have. He can sit and concentrate on something with a crowd of people sitting around him, and never hear a word they say. He tunes everything out, keeping his mind directly on what he feels is most important. I'm not that way. If there's a radio or a television set on, I can't concentrate. I can't even have music on if I'm trying to concentrate.

However, there are times when I need to

stop and create an atmosphere of worship in our home. If I'm absolutely alone and don't have a pressing task to do, I put on some good Christian records and get my Bible, and really have an hour of worship. Christian music does something to me. It puts me in the mood to talk to the Lord and to listen to Him.

I wrote to a boy recently who said he was at the point where he wanted to commit suicide. He felt he was being discriminated against because he was Black and he had not been able to cope with this.

I told him something my husband has said many times — no matter what color or what race we are, we are unique and irreplaceable in God's eyes. We need to recognize that God thinks we are valuable beyond price.

In my quiet time, God shows me that I'm valuable to Him. He sets my thinking straight, and I become convinced anew that discouragement and weariness come from Satan. It is his work to kill and destroy — not the Lord's. The Lord uplifts, and He wants us to live abundantly.

The next time you have a discouraging

day, why not get alone for a few minutes with your Bible and God. Maybe there's a special place you can go — maybe it's just out for a walk. Pause to remember that *you* are valuable beyond price. Nobody is more important to God than you are. And remember, too, that tomorrow is a new day.

Doing those things makes the busy days of *my* life easier to handle for me, and I believe they will also work for you.

Back on TV

Being on television is *not* my cup of tea. One of the most difficult things for me to do is to make television appearances. I'd much rather stand beside Oral with my faith and prayers and stand *behind* the camera while I'm praying!

It was never my desire to take a part in the television ministry. I am not a public person. I don't have any desire to be. But seven years ago, when we started the new format for the television ministry, Oral began saying to me, "Now, Evelyn, I want you to get involved in this."

I'd always respond, "Oral, just let me sit in a room with a monitor so I can watch you and I'll do anything I can to help *you*. I'll suggest things to you when I think you can do better. But please don't ask me to go in front of that camera because I'll freeze."

More than twenty years ago, our first television experience was in Hollywood. The format was much like that of our radio program. Oral would walk in and sit on a couch in a living room set and I would read testimonies the same way I read them for the radio programs. It was a very stilted program. I was not natural at all.

On radio, with a microphone in front of me and nobody watching, I could be my normal self. But in front of that camera, I absolutely froze. I could not do a thing. I looked a million years old because I was so tense and stiff. I knew that television was *not* my medium.

I kept thinking about "all those people," and Oral kept telling me during these years, "Evelyn, the Lord can help you with this. There is a ministry for you to perform if you will just have faith in yourself."

Well, I didn't have any faith in myself — not for television! He kept telling me that I could do it and I kept telling him I could not. It was a real tug of war. I knew I was valuable when it came to cooking and washing and ironing. I knew God could answer prayers to help Oral. But when it came to being in public, I just didn't have any confidence in myself. I didn't think I had anything valuable to contribute.

Of course, Oral is quite insistent — and very *persistent*. He decided himself to bring me on a little at a time. He'd ask me to read just a letter with him or pray with him or sit with the children in a background group shot.

Finally, he said to me, "Honey, just think of that camera as being some lonely woman sitting in an apartment all alone. Speak only to her. Or think about a family sitting in their living room — a family that really needs to hear the gospel. Imagine a person or a family. Don't think about the mass of people."

And that seemed to click in my mind and heart. I love to talk with individuals and small groups and families. Suddenly, television took on a new meaning for me. It meant a chance to share with a *person,* not an *audience.* I began to relax and think about people instead of cameras.

So Oral gets the credit, or the blame, for my being on the programs because he just would not let me say no. He kept after me until I had no way to escape.

And now I'm really glad he did. Television has now become so comfortable to me, I find I'm now trying to help *Oral* relax! That's really a switch!

But even more important than being able to share in the television ministry, I'm grateful to Oral for making me feel as if I have something valuable to share. He gave me a very special feeling. He saw in me a potential I couldn't see. He encouraged me to become all I could become, by God's help. He made me realize that I am important to him as a person — not because I can cook and iron shirts, but because I am who I am. I think every husband can make his wife feel that way, and vice versa.

Returning to television was not only a personal challenge in our ministry; it opened new doors of opportunity — and struggles always seem to come with opportunity.

When the World Action Singers joined us on television as regular performers, many people in the church world, and some outside the church, felt we had added dancers to our program. They thought the students should stand very still and not carry on such an unholy way. If Oral sees church people standing absolutely still, he says, "Oh, why don't church people look alive, use their talents for the Lord in the same way others use their talents for the devil. People are alive and have *life,* and Christians, especially, should *look* like it."

Before we knew it, musicians on other church programs were also infusing some life into their singing — and to me, their programs are more exciting for it.

Many of our specials have been produced "on location" — in England, Japan, Alaska, and Hawaii. I believe the conditions under which we worked at the World Expo in Japan were the most difficult we've ever experienced in producing a special. The language barrier was a great handicap and there were many other hindrances. In fact, if God had not worked some miracles, our program could never have been finished.

The heat and humidity were the worst we've ever faced in any nation. One day while Richard, Patti, and the Singers were working out in the sun, one of our girls fainted and the others began to get sick. We had to stop the cameras, pray with the students, and let them rest before we could continue.

Many technical difficulties arose. Our producer said, "The first day, the language barrier and technical procedures were so tough, I really began to think we had wasted our trip. Then I realized that God knew all about these things months before when He had impressed us to come, and He would be our answer. Also, I remember that Oral had said many times that Christ is always at the point of our need and He comes to us in the form of that need. I relaxed and soon we were able to communicate with our Japanese cameramen. All of them were experts and once the communication barrier was overcome, things went more smoothly."

And you know, the number of people who were blessed during that special far exceeded the number during any other program we had produced up to that time.

As can be expected, the expense of producing television programs is enormous. When Oral told me about his plans to return to television with one-hour quarterly specials and half-hour weekly programs, the immensity of it scared me half to death. We just didn't have the money — in fact, it seemed to take all our faith just to keep the university and the ministry going. I thought of the continuous struggle we would have with television stations to sell us time. I thought of the cost and the possibility of failure. To return to TV was truly a step of faith. But I sensed, as Oral shared with me, that he had heard from God, and we moved ahead.

I praise God often for the miracle of financial support that has arisen to keep our programs on the air. We are now putting television tapes of Oral's programs and lectures, and Bibles into prisons across America. Believe with us that God will bless this new facet of our television ministry! Also, Oral's lectures on the Holy Spirit have been video-taped, and American cable stations and television stations in other countries have begun to request these programs for airing in many cities. The opportunities are overtaking the struggles.

We are now producing our television

programs at ORU. ORU people help us direct and edit the programs, and more and more ORU students and faculty members are taking a part. We have a new "look" and we have exciting things planned ahead.

Will you pray with us that God will use Oral's sermons to bless people across this land? And if you come to Tulsa when we are taping programs, I hope you'll check to see how you can be a part of our audiences. Each TV taping is done before a live audience; we think we can communicate better this way. Sometimes the anointing is so heavy, even the cameramen feel it. It's exciting to think that what you feel in your soul can come across to a person watching a TV set.

We believe God can use television in working miracles. And those miracles are happening! Our mail tells us so. People we meet all across the land tell us.

One day, Oral and I were driving through a city and he noticed a TV aerial on top of every house we passed. After a while he said, "Thousands of them."

"Thousands of what?"

"Thousands of TV homes. And just

think, nearly every one of them tunes us in at one time or another."

I said, "It means a lot to you, doesn't it, Honey?"

"Yes," he replied, "but think of how much more it means to God."

Then he added, "Evelyn, as Christians we must not grow stale or permit any part of our TV program to be less than God's best. We may be the only ones in the whole world touching some of the people in those homes with God's healing power."

It's times like this that I sense the importance of a man gifted of God . . . and whether or not he's using his gifts to uplift people. The times when I've been short-tempered with Oral, or have felt resentment at his pushing me to use my talents, come to mind. His "pushing" now gives meaning to my life. Every TV aerial assumes human shape, a life, a soul. I steal a glance at my husband and thank God I'm married to a man of God — and that man is Oral Roberts.

New Sons and Daughters

There couldn't be a mother-in-law more proud than I am of the mates my children have chosen.

As they were growing up, I often wondered how I could ever trust them into someone else's care and how I would feel when the time came for them to establish homes of their own.

Marshall Nash was the first "new son" to venture into our lives. When he came to our home to ask for permission for Rebecca to be his wife, he was so nervous, we couldn't get him to sit down, so he stood. After Oral and I agreed and he relaxed, I remember saying to him, "Marshall, do you love Rebecca enough to live with her all your life?"

"Yes, I do. In fact, I can't live without her."

"Well, I'm glad, because if you take her, you can't bring her back. Be very sure. We don't get divorces in our family. Marriage is for life — and life is a long time." His brown eyes snapped, and I could see the determination in them. (Rebecca had already told me she was in love with the most fabulous man in the world — and I said, ". . . besides your dad.")

They've been married eighteen years — beautiful years. Marshall has a great business ability and we are pleased that he has coupled this driving ambition with absolute honesty. We couldn't have put our daughter into better hands.

Ronnie had always been an individualist, and Oral and I were prepared to accept and love any girl he might choose. But I do admit to much prayer concerning the right wife for him.

And wouldn't you know, he picked Carol Croskery — a lovely girl from Tulsa whom we had known since their high school days together. Now, isn't that just like the Lord?

It had to be the Lord because Ronnie had been stationed in California during his army career and then transferred to the east coast, where Carol was teaching school.

Carol and Ronnie had given their first flute recital together. And many afternoons after school, they sat in our den with a glass of milk and cookies, listening to records or tapes.

Carol and Oral and I had a good talk together when she and Ronnie came home from the east coast for the wedding. I said to her, "Carol, you've known us casually for years, but do you really know what we think and believe?"

She said, "Oh, yes, of course I know. And I want you both to know that I am marrying Ronnie not only because I love him. I *do* love him, but there is a compelling force that tells me I *must* marry him."

Carol finished her bachelor's degree and received her master's degree at Peabody School of Music. She now teaches flute at ORU. It's difficult for me to realize they've been married for ten years, because they lived out of state for so long. These past four years since they have been in Tulsa Oral and I have grown to appreciate Carol even more — for what she is and for what she means to Ronnie and our whole family. She is a precious girl and we love her.

When Richard first told me that he had a date with Patti Holcomb, I had two fears. First, I felt Patti had the best singing voice on campus, and I feared Richard might be attracted only to her voice. My second fear was that she was too mature for him. She had traveled overseas with a well-known singing group before coming to ORU as one of the first freshmen in 1965. By the time Richard met her, she was a junior in college and he was a sophomore.

But I knew human nature well enough to know that if I pointed out these things to Richard, he'd probably be more attracted to her than ever — so I decided to tell the Lord my fears and just sit back and see what would happen.

After they had dated for a semester, Patti left for Europe with our first group of World Action Singers and Richard stayed in Tulsa to work on a radio station. He was so lonely, my heart ached for him. I began to realize how much Patti meant to him.

Oral and I were to join the group in England and go on to Israel and Africa with them. While I was packing to leave, Richard said, "Mother, will you take something to Patti for me?"

I said, "Of course, what is it?"

It was a can of Dr. Pepper. On the can he had written, "As often as you drink of this, think of me."

In Europe, Patti and I had many opportunities to get to know each other. She told me her dreams, her hopes, and her aspirations. I realized she had a deep faith — much deeper than I had suspected. One day she said to me, "Mrs. Roberts, I think I love your son."

"Patti," I said, "be sure. I don't want either of you to make a mistake."

More people know Patti than any other of our children's spouses because of her television appearances. But few know what a warmhearted person she is and how much we love her. Patti and I are very close. We not only work closely together, we are very compatible and enjoy many of the same things.

Ron Potts, Roberta's husband, is one of five children, all of whom have attended Oral Roberts University. He is the son of a minister in Iowa. When he began to date Roberta, he was very shy about coming to our home because he was afraid if the word got out on campus that he was dating the president's daughter, he would never hear the end of it.

Roberta is a very affectionate person — much like her father — and she loves people so much, I had a fear that she couldn't distinguish romantic love from her *general* love for everybody. I knew Roberta *thought* she loved him, but she had *thought* she loved others before. I questioned her a great deal to find out what her true feelings were. I began to notice, too, that her outlook on life was much brighter when Ron was around, and that she tended to be bored with life when he wasn't near.

Finally, they came to us and told us they wanted to be married. They were juniors at ORU and I thought they should finish school first — but that wasn't their plan.

Ron came to me one day and said, "Mrs. Roberts, I really love Roberta."

"Ron, I'm not sure she knows what she wants. She's a person who gets tired of people easily. She has an inquiring mind and unless life is full of action, she's easily bored."

"Well, I believe I can cope with her."

"Okay, Ron. But remember — make up your mind before you marry her because once you take her she's yours for life. There are no divorces in our family."

(Perhaps I stressed this too much with my children and their mates, but divorce was such a traumatic event in my own life as a child, I don't want my children or grandchildren to experience it. Now, they all may divorce tomorrow, but it won't be because I neglected to give them my opinion.)

They were married by Rev. Oscar Moore, the same minister who said the ceremony for Oral and me thirty-nine years ago.

Ron has been very good to Roberta during the six years they've been married. He's even-tempered and comfortable to be around. He and I have a rapport which, I believe, began with our first talk together.

After he and Roberta married, he wasn't interested in finishing his degree. He thought he should drop out of college and get a full-time job. I'm sure he grew weary of my nagging him, but every time he spoke to me about quitting, I'd say, "Ron, remember you promised me you'd finish school."

"But, Evelyn," he would say (all of our children-in-law call us Oral and Evelyn), "I don't need a degree. I don't plan to teach." (He was a physical education major.)

"But, Ron, suppose you want to be a coach. You can't do it without a degree." So I nagged and nagged until he went down that aisle in his cap and gown right beside Roberta. Two proud parents — besides Oral and me — watched him that day . . . his parents.

We love Ron, and thank Jesus for giving him to Roberta to be a part of our family.

Oral and I are so very grateful that all of our children and their spouses have embraced the Seed-Faith way of life. They all are givers to the Lord's work.

Each couple has sponsored an ORU project and each has told us of the ways in which God is multiplying back into their lives "the seed sown."

Munna and Andy

I believe the greatest reward of motherhood has been to see my children living meaningful Christian lives, happily married and settled in homes of their own with their little families.

It is still hard for me to believe that Rebecca, our eldest, has a daughter who will soon be a teen-ager. Brenda Ann Nash, our first granddaughter, was born the year before ORU began — 1964. She was the pride and joy of my heart — a beautiful baby — and I was always ready to show her off. She was, and is, very special to me.

I'd heard people say that you're closer to your grandchildren than to your children. I never believed that until Brenda came. She was as close to me as if she were my own. Richard and Roberta were still at home then and when Rebecca would leave town or have errands to do, she would often bring Brenda to the house. I was with her more and able to keep her more often than any of our other grandchildren since, and I enjoyed her so much.

I wanted to teach her to call me "Grandmother" and to call Oral "Granddaddy." Those were the names I had for my grandparents. I'd say to Brenda, "Now Brenda, I am Grandmother." Before she was old enough to talk I'd say, "Let Grandmother do this for you," "Let Grandmother do that for you," "Let Granddaddy do so-and-so. . . ."

When she began trying to say Grandmother, it turned out "Danmunna." When she tried to say Granddaddy, it was too big for her; it turned out "Dandaddy." Finally, she created her own words, "Munna" and "Andy."

When Brenda was about two, she was visiting at our house one night and Oral said to me, "Do you suppose that when this child is grown up she'll say grandmother and granddaddy?" He didn't think Brenda heard him, but she immediately looked up and said, "No, it will be Munna and

Andy." And it has been Munna and Andy for every one of our grandchildren. I'm not a grandmother, and I never will be. I'm Munna.

Rather sheepishly, Oral once told some men at NBC, "If you hear anybody yell Munna and Andy, let me know. It will be two of my grandchildren who are going to be on one of our programs."

Marcia Elaine Nash was the second grandchild. Now, Brenda is a young lady in the finest sense of the word. She is very reserved; she crossed her legs when she sat down and pulled her dress down over her knees even as a little girl. Marcia was a tomboy to the nth degree — a completely different personality — but so lovable and adorable. Just a look and a smile, and she's captured you. But she'll knock your block off if she has half a chance!

One day I was baby-sitting with Marcia, who wanted to be told a story. Marcia loves Bible stories so I told her about the birth of the baby Jesus, His life and ministry after He grew into manhood, and finally about His death on the cross, and His resurrection.

When I finished, Marcia pleaded, "Tell me another story."

"Well, Honey, what would you like to hear about now?"

"Tell me the rest of Jesus," she said.

It's amazing to me how different all of my grandchildren are. Little Jon, Rebecca's third child, was the first grandson in the family. We could hardly wait for him to walk and talk. We practically forced him to grow up. He is a beautiful child with jet-black curly hair and brown eyes.

I always wanted one of my children to have brown eyes because Oral is the only blue-eyed child in his family. All the rest of his brothers and sisters have brown eyes. Mama Roberts, though, prayed for a blue-eyed child and had one — Oral. So I wanted a child in my family to resemble the rest of the Roberts family. And I didn't have a single brown-eyed child. Then Jon came along. They named him Jon Oral after his grandfather, and he has the prettiest brown eyes you've ever seen.

Richard and Patti were married a couple of years before they thought about having children. Then it looked as if they weren't going to be able to have a baby, so they filed for adoption. They went to several agencies and it seemed they were going to have to wait quite a while.

But I know God knew how much they wanted a baby because He led them to the child that is the light of our lives. Richard called me one afternoon and said, "Mother, you're going to become a new grandmother about six o'clock."

I said, "Are you really going to get the baby that soon?"

"Yes, would you like to go with us to the airport?"

"No, because you'll be so nervous, I'd be scared to ride in a car you are driving. Now, Richard, be careful and don't kill that baby before you get home with her. Call me the moment you're home, and we'll be there immediately."

About six fifteen he called again and said, "Mother, you and Dad can come over and see your new granddaughter, Christine Michelle." When I walked into their house, Patti was sitting in a little blue rocking chair giving the baby a bottle. I shall never forget what a picture she made. She had the most satisfied look on her face that I've ever seen.

I have to be honest and say that Oral and I were a little afraid that we might not feel the same way about this child as we felt toward the children who were born into our family. But the moment we saw that baby and held her in our arms, she was ours, a part of us. Oral took Christi on his lap and looked at her and said, "Something went through me, and I know this child is ours as much as any child that has been born into our family." It was a moving experience for all of us.

Richard and Patti were so excited, they called everybody immediately. Ronnie and Carol were so excited, too! They had wanted a child for more than four years. And naturally, while they rejoiced at Richard and Patti's being so blessed, they were envious.

But God had a miracle for them, too. Only a month later, Ronnie and Carol became the parents of five-day-old Rachel Ellen. And it was just like having my own baby all over again.

I remember so well a story that Tommy

Tyson tells about having visited in the home of some friends. He noticed that they paid particular attention to every whim of their child. When Tommy was ready to leave, the father picked up the little girl and said, "Honey, tell Brother Tommy what kind of a child you are."

"I am a chosen child," she said.

And that's how I feel about these children — they are chosen, just as the Bible says, "Ye have not chosen me, but I have chosen you." (John 15:16)

We feel our family has been very blessed with Christi and Rachel. We are convinced the Lord arranged it just as it is.

About a year after Christi was adopted, Patti and Richard had little Juline Allison. Juli had the funny little upturned Roberts nose that all of my babies had. She has the sweetest laugh. Both girls enjoy each other so much, being only eleven months apart.

Christi is fascinated with the story of her adoption. She always says, "Mommy, tell me about how the airplane brought me."

One day, I said to her, "Christi, *you* tell me about how the airplane brought you."

And she said, "Well, my mommy had

something wrong with her tummy and she couldn't have children, so she had to get me from someplace besides the hospital. And an airplane flew right in and a man had me wrapped in a blanket and he just put me in Mommy's arms. And Mommy brought me home, and I'm her little girl.''

One day, Christi came over for a few hours. Her mommy and daddy were gone and she called me and said, ''Munna, could I please spend some time with you?''

And I said, ''Yes. Would you like to come over and have lunch with me?''

She said, ''Yes, and supper, too.''

So she came over. She had it fixed in her mind what she wanted to do. She wanted take-out chicken for dinner and she wanted to eat it here. To her, that was eating in a ''westerant.''

Afterward, we had a few errands to do and I said, ''Christi, I'd like to go over here and look at a mattress for a baby bed.''

The mattress on my old baby bed we had for our grandchildren was worn out after eleven years' use. Christi looked up at me with the cutest wide-eyed look and said,

"Munna, are *you* having a baby?"

Our last two grandchildren were boys. Ronnie and Carol's second child, Damon Wingate Croskery-Roberts, is our only grandson to date with the name Roberts. He is such a sweet, lovable, good baby, and is just now beginning to walk and to talk.

Roberta's little boy, Randall Roberts Potts, will always be extremely close to us because he lives just down the street. He can get by me with almost anything, except turning the dial on my dishwasher!

And to every one of them, I'm Munna. When I call Ronnie and Carol's, Rachel sometimes answers the phone and she says, "This is Rachel Ellen Croskery-Roberts."

And I say, "Is this Rachel Ellen Croskery-Roberts?"

And she'll say, "Oh, it's Munna, Mommy. It's Munna."

This brings to mind the Christmas TV special we did when most of the grandchildren were babies. There was a nursery scene with each mother standing by her own child's crib. In order to catch them in a natural pose, we had to keep them on camera much longer than we wanted to — shooting the scene again and again.

Rachel was about two, but she could say quite a few words. After Oral had kissed her about six times and was about to kiss her again, she said, "Andy, go away! I don't like you anymore."

My ambition as a grandmother is to share Jesus with each one of my grandchildren. I love to tell them Bible stories and teach them songs about Jesus.

Several years ago, I gave each grandchild a tape for Christmas. On the tape I sang some songs for them, told the Bible story of Jesus and His birth, and explained what Christmas was all about. Not long ago, Jon came over with his tape recorder. He said excitedly, "Munna, you're *singing* on my tape."

"I am?"

"Yes, I want to play it for you." He played it, and there I was, singing those little Christmas songs to him.

Rebecca said he carries that tape recorder all over the house with him, singing along with me. He's learned all the songs.

Having seen Jon with his tape recorder,

I asked Christi one day, "Christi, do you still have your tape recorder that Munna gave you for Christmas?"

"Yes."

"Do you ever listen to it?"

"Yes."

"Can you tell me one of the songs that I sang?"

And she sang, "Dashing through the snow, in a one horse open sleigh. . . ."

They don't forget a thing. One thing I hope they'll always remember is that Munna and Andy believe in a good God who loves them and wants to be their friend.

Today and Tomorrow

I'm a calm-natured woman who likes to find a nice, comfortable rut and stay in it. Oral Roberts is exactly the opposite. So, life has been exciting because Oral has never allowed me to die while I live.

I've never given a second thought to growing old, because of Oral. He won't let me grow old. He will not allow it. If I mention that I have arthritis in my little finger, he says, "Don't mention that word in this house. We're not negative in this house and you're not going to have arthritis. Don't say that word in this house." If I say that my bones ache, he'll say, "Oh, Evelyn, get up and stand up straight. Stand up on the inside and we'll talk to the Lord about this. You're not growing old. I want you to know that. No matter how old you are chronologically, you don't have to be old in your mind and in your spirit."

Recently, some students brought out a rocker for me to sit in during an ORU chapel. I had told them how I had looked forward to retirement, but that I feared I'd never have the chance to "sit back and relax in a rocker." So they surprised me with a rocker.

But do you think Oral would let me sit in that rocker while he preached? Not a chance. When he got up to speak, he looked over at me and said, "Evelyn, please get out of that rocker and sit in a straight chair, or I can't preach." The students just howled with laughter. He told me later it made me look old, and he wasn't about to stand for that.

Mama Roberts believed that, "If we love Jesus, we're young at heart." Oral believes the same way and he makes sure I do, too.

I'm in excellent health, and I owe my good health in part to aerobics and to the positive attitude of the man I live with.

I walk one and a half miles many days on the indoor track of ORU's Aerobic Center. Sometimes, students walk along with me and ask me questions or share things with me. But if nobody walks with me and I'm alone, I use that time for talking to the Lord. You don't have to move your lips to talk to God, you know. It's an especially good time to use the prayer language of the Spirit.

It takes me twenty-five minutes to walk a mile and a half, and that's a good long time to talk to the Lord. Not only do I feel younger and have more vitality and more strength, I come away spiritually refreshed.

I believe that the Lord gave us our physical bodies and that we are to take care of them as we care for our minds and souls. The body was the first part of us that God made. He breathed His Spirit into us only after He made our bodies as vessels. I don't think the Lord wants us to let His creation deteriorate.

Recently, I've found prayer sweeter than ever. When my husband goes up in the Prayer Tower to be alone with God, it does me almost as much good as it does him. I have my own prayer time. Prayer opens me up inside, turns me upward toward God and outward toward people. I thank God for the privilege of prayer. It's a direct line to our Father in heaven Who is concerned about every child of His on earth.

Mama Roberts once said, "Oral, you don't have to know how to pray. All you have to do is open your heart and tell God all about it, and He will do the rest."

I taught my children, "Just say it to God as you feel it and mean it. Say, 'Dear God, this is what I feel in my heart,' or, 'Jesus, I love You,' Or, 'Jesus, I know that You know all about this.' "

Jesus didn't pray that God would take us out of the world, but that He would "keep" us in this world.

Oral believes in going into every man's world. If he had listened to me, I'm afraid we would have stayed pretty much in our own little world with all of our associates and church people. I don't enjoy being among people with whom I have little in common, but I know Oral is right. When we attend parties in other people's worlds, the Lord is brought invariably into our conversations and people often pour out problems to us.

The average minister takes care of his

flock and has someone else to do the business part of his job. Oral has had to be involved in the world of business as much as the world of religion. We have met many wonderful people, many of them in the business world who are interested in God. But we have also been thrown into contact with some people who are heavy drinkers.

I have had to pray a great deal about my prejudice against people who drink. It has been difficult for me to tolerate a person who gets drunk, and to separate the drunks from the drunkenness. Alcohol broke up my home when I was four, and I am adamant in my opinion about drinking.

At a big party one evening, a leader in our community came over to me, introduced himself, and then asked me to dance. I've never been drunk myself, but I've seen enough drunks to know he had had one too many. I'm afraid my respect for him dropped to zero, even before our conversation.

Inside myself, I was crying, "Oral, where are you? Rescue me from this wretched creature."

I managed to be kind, but firm, and moved away from him and almost immediately saw Oral come toward me.

In the car on the way home, I said, "Oral, I almost blew my stack tonight at a man. . . ."

"Why, what did he do?"

"He persistently asked me to dance, and of course I told him I don't dance. But the part that bothered me most was his drunken condition. Oral, I can't stand that man. And anyway, where were *you?* Why did you leave me for so long?"

"Now, Evelyn, you can hate the drunkenness, but not the man. He needs the Lord and he needs your prayers — not your hatred."

God does not tolerate the sin, but loves the sinner. I know this and I really have to pray very hard to be more like Jesus.

I suppose the greatest relaxation of my life is just to be alone with Oral. Sometimes we like to take long walks and just talk.

Sometimes, when we have a free evening, we go out to dinner with friends. Many times, we have our children over. Sometimes we visit them at their homes in the evenings, or use our evenings to prepare for a seminar or meeting; we'll toss ideas back and forth. Sometimes, we'll just spend an evening reading or exercising.

I try to do everything I can to help Oral relax. He especially enjoys having friends over for a whole evening of relaxed conversation. He likes to have our coaches come and discuss athletics. But we don't really need people in order to live. We enjoy being together, just the two of us.

We'll never run out of things to talk about because Oral has so many ideas about the future of ORU and our lives together in this ministry. We have to talk about plans ten years from now!

If we go to a big city, I love to browse through second-hand book stores for old books that aren't on the market any more. Years ago, when we'd go to New York City, I'd go alone to antique shops and old stores. I didn't purchase very much, but I enjoyed looking.

Now, if I have a free day, I enjoy going to look at homes and flowers, scenery, museums, places of interest in other cities, and things like that. I love to go to arts-

and-crafts shows. I love to see what people have made with their own hands.

I enjoy handwork. I'm taking up needlepoint right now. I've always done a lot of crocheting, crewel embroidery, and regular embroidery. I used to do some tatting when I was young. I enjoy collecting recipes, too. I'm just a born collector.

Now that the children are grown, I have more time to spend in public speaking. Just recently, I spoke to 235 women in Chicago. And, as I write this, I have just finished speaking to 3,500 women who attended the Ladies Luncheon of the International Convention of the Full Gospel Business Men's Fellowship.

Public speaking is something that I've had to *learn* to do. I was always comfortable in a teaching situation where I had a book in front of me and could refer to it. But Oral never preaches with notes and he thinks I should speak without notes, too. He believes if a person has anything worth saying, it's worth studying enough beforehand so he doesn't need notes. For the speeches I give, the most difficult part is spending enough time studying and researching.

Oral has begun to chide me a bit and say, "Evelyn, you study more for a speech than I do for a sermon."

And I say, "Now whose fault do you suppose that is? You want me to speak without notes, and yet you don't want me to study."

"No, it isn't that I don't want you to study, I just think it's funny — you spend half your day studying for a speech."

Last September, Oral said to me, "Evelyn, I want you to become involved this year with the students, more than you've ever been. I want you to spend more time on campus."

So I began to get more involved in student Bible studies and I spoke to several student groups. Soon Oral began saying to me, "Now where are you going tonight?"

"I'm going to the campus."

"You have to make a speech *again* tonight?"

"Yes."

"Who this time — students? Well, what am *I* going to do this evening?"

The speeches became more and more

frequent, and he said, "Evelyn, you're making an awful lot of speeches and I don't enjoy being left here alone."

"Now whose fault do you suppose that is? You told me last September to get involved. You weren't happy until I did and now that I'm involved, you're not happy. So what am I to do?"

"Well, I just don't want you to be *that* involved."

Oral is willing to liberate me as long as it doesn't interfere with his comfort. He's always said to me, "You can go and make a speech out of town if you can get back before bedtime!"

With all there is to do, I never have time to be bored. I have goals and a purpose in my life. And to me, that's important for all of us — no matter what our age or occupation.

I believe we have to stay busy working for the Lord to counteract all the negative things in our world today.

We live in a negative age.

Any time of the day, you can turn on the radio and hear about the energy crisis, the bad weather, the investigation of a political figure, gasoline prices going up, food prices skyrocketing.

Everything seems to be negative. Nothing sounds positive.

Without God as the center of our lives, it could get frustrating trying to make dollars go farther, to keep children free from illnesses, to save on doctors' bills.

Recently, Oral and I were out of the city doing television programs and I didn't go to a grocery store for several weeks. When I returned, I was shocked to see the higher prices. I came home sputtering to Oral, "My goodness! If it's hard for me to buy for just us two, how do people who have four or five children manage?"

The outlook on our lives seems very dark, and there is much pessimism. But there's a brighter side, too! I think we need to concentrate on that.

I believe there is a move back to God. Not only by young people, but also by parents. In the last several years, little groups of people have begun meeting to find out what the Scriptures say. These people never really desired to know before. I believe as they find out what's in the

Bible, the whole mood of the country will change. I think it's already changing.

I really do give the young people much of the credit for starting this new move of the Spirit. Parents have begun to be aware that the restlessness of their children was brought on by a desire for something spiritual, a hunger for Jesus that they did not know how to label.

About the time the Jesus Movement began among young people, the power of the Holy Spirit began to move in virtually all the churches. These movements have spread into our homes. Homes are changing and in the next few years, I think we are going to see a great, overall change in America.

I believe the stage is being set for a great event in world history.

Two or three times recently, I've been approached with the question: "Mrs. Roberts, what do you think is going to happen next in this world?" It gives me an opportunity to say, "I think the coming of the Lord is going to be next."

What do I mean by "the coming of the Lord"? Do I think the Lord is actually coming here in person? I definitely think the Bible teaches that.

I seldom have dreams that seem worthwhile, but many years ago I had a dream that was very real and very special to me.

I dreamed that Oral and I had taken Rebecca, Ronnie, and Richard to church. Roberta was asleep in her crib and I had left her at home.

As we started into the church, Oral and I simultaneously looked up at the sky and then at each other. The sky was changing colors like a rainbow and both of us said at the same time, "Jesus is coming." There was a hush — as if the elements of the earth were waiting breathlessly.

We stepped inside a Sunday school room at the side of the church, waiting for the Lord to come. In a moment of time, He came right through the ceiling and stood before us in a gleaming white robe. He looked over our little family and smiled. We gathered as close to Him as we could get, telling Him how much we loved Him, and He answered, "Yes, I love you, too." I remember I walked up and looked into

His face and said, "Jesus, don't go away without us, take us all with you." He smiled.

Then He told us to go on into the church. When we went in, the service had already begun. Apparently, no one else had seen Jesus.

In a few moments, I looked around, and there beside us sat Jesus, dressed as an ordinary man. He was just sitting there, observing the service.

All of a sudden, I remembered Roberta at home asleep. I wanted to go get her, but was afraid Jesus would leave while I was gone. So I slipped over beside Him and said, "Jesus, I would like to go home for my baby; please don't leave without us."

He smiled and said, "Go and get her." I shall never forget that smile as long as I live.

At this point, I awoke from my dream. It had been so real, I reached over to see if Oral was still there.

The world *is* coming to an end. The Bible says it is. The Bible tells us that God is going to removate this earth. The evil in the earth will be destroyed by fire, but the earth itself will not be destroyed. God is going to renovate it and there will be a new heaven and a new earth, and this is where He intends for us to live.

But first there's going to be a sifting of people.

Jesus has promised that when He comes, He will put the sheep on the right and the goats on the left. And I always tell people, you need not be overly concerned about what's going to happen in the world if you're ready for the coming of the Lord. That's the first thing we have to be concerned about. If you're sure that you have a personal and warm relationship with God and you know Jesus Christ as your Lord and Savior, then you are ready to meet Him. You don't have to worry about what the Lord is going to do next or when the judgment is coming. God will take care of you.

I don't worry about the future. I work to know that I'm prepared to meet the Lord when He calls for me.

It's beautiful how God knows the end from the beginning. We often wonder why He doesn't roll the curtain back and let us see our future, but I'm sure He loves us too much to do that. I'm looking forward to the day I can be with Him . . . forever.

Still a Call

One day, I asked, "Oral, when are you going to quit?"

He looked very seriously at me and said, "Never, Evelyn. As long as the Lord has work for me, I'm going to do it. As long as there are people in the world starving for the Word, I can't settle down. I wouldn't be happy."

I know my husband. He wouldn't be happy even *slowing* down.

Just recently, Oral revealed some of the things God had ordered him to do at ORU. By 1978, ORU is to have a Christian medical school and dental school, and by 1979, a law school. Before he made the announcement to the students and faculty, he presented these plans to the Board of Regents.

I wrote in my diary:

10:20 A.M.

Saturday, April 26, 1975

Oral has just left for a meeting with the executive committee of ORU's board of regents. There's an urgency in his spirit because God has said *now* is the time to make plans to launch a program for the school of medicine at ORU. I have no doubt this is the biggest task yet that God has given him to do.

Since 1962 or 1963, Oral has been mentioning casually to his friends that a school of medicine was in his long-range planning. I didn't give it much thought until about two years ago when he told me, "Evelyn, God is getting ready to do something so much greater than He has ever done through me, and I'm really scared." And then he said to me, "Evelyn, I have to obey Him. I have no choice."

Oral began walking the floor at night praying, crying, and reading his Bible, just as he did in 1947 when he began the healing ministry, and again in the early 1960's when ORU was about to be born.

He has said many times recently, "Evelyn, this is a baby trying to be born. I'm going through the birth pangs, and I know it."

For over a year now, he and the board of regents have had a special committee doing research on medical schools. They've visited schools across the country, reporting their findings to Oral.

Logic says it can't be done. Well, this isn't new. Some people have always said, "It can't be done," to things God has told Oral to do. And I know that when the news hits the newspapers, our enemies will come out of the woods. We both know this, but we both know a greater truth: *He that is in us is greater than he that is in the world.*

I admit this is a job that I don't look forward to, because I'm tired of struggle. It would be so easy now, at age fifty-eight, to sit back, relax, do some needlepoint, enjoy my grandchildren, and watch the students of ORU develop into beautiful, worthwhile citizens who will go out and change the world. But I know, too, when you sit down, you die.

Oral said to me this morning, "Evelyn, I'd like a few minutes of your time."

I said, "Okay, what can I do for you?"

He said, "Honey, I feel a need for prayer before I go to meet the exective committee."

"All right, Oral. May I play a tape for you first?"

"Yes."

So I put on a videotape of one of our half-hour television programs in which he and I discussed III John 2. Patti sang, "Jesus, Jesus," and Richard sang, "How Big Is God."

Both of us sat and cried and prayed together. When God is focused in a true perspective in our lives, everything else falls into place.

Oral left, lifted up in his spirit, with tears in his eyes. God's will *shall* be done. It is not ours to question how — *I just know* that I know that I know that I know.

My high school superintendent had a favorite saying: "No one has a right to die without leaving something for the next generation." His saying has stayed with me. I have asked myself many times, "What contribution am I making to the next generation? When I am gone, will they say, 'The world is better because she lived in it,' or will they say, 'She lived a selfish life and we're better off now that she's gone'?"

I know our future is in God's hands. I want to do all I can to stay in His will and work for Him. I'll quit when Oral quits — *never!*

The publishers hope that this Large Print Book has brought you pleasurable reading. Each title is designed to make the text as easy to see as possible. G. K. Hall Large Print Books are available only from your library or through the Large Print Book Club. If you wish a complete list of the Large Print Books we have published or information about our Book Club, please write directly to:

G. K. Hall & Co.
70 Lincoln Street
Boston, Mass. 02111